"While the author cautions readers not to use this book for self-help purposes, one of the most powerful messages that we receive from reading it is the unlocking of our lives that can occur from the decision to actively seek therapy – the most important of which is to unlock the potential for happiness in life. For so many people, psychotherapy is a dark unknown that seems mysterious and without definition. This book demystifies the therapeutic journey and provides a compelling argument for seeking assistance and support in times of trouble. As a lifelong educator, I have counseled many people – at all ages – to seek help. In the future, I will recommend *Between the Lines* to provide concrete and inspiring examples of how happiness can be found!"

Jay Lewis
Middle School and High School Principal: 1983-2010
Associate Dean, School of Education, Hofstra University: 2010-present

"Between the Lines is a clear, straightforward and honest guide to Cognitive Behavioral Therapy that weaves together important insights needed to cope in the postmodern world: the deep impact of rapid cultural change on the American family since the 1950s; the confusion of identity and destruction of family boundaries that foster dysfunction, dependency and harm; the mass denial that feeds immobility and dread; the mechanics of victimization; the destructive effects of stress on physical and mental functioning; and the central importance of a cognitive and behavioral approach that recasts deep suppositions so to liberate the individual from a cul-de-sac of pain and despair. Doctor Guido's case study infuses his argument with deep emotion and his honest self-disclosure imbues the book with rare authenticity."

Rocco Lo Bosco
Co-author of Going Crooked: A Psychoanalytic Perspective on
Perversion, Technology and Society, author Buddha
Wept and Ninety-Nine

"Have you ever felt 'stuck' — paralyzed by fear, not your 'old self,' and unable to overcome obstacles that are keeping you from peace of mind and productive, balanced relationships? If so, this remarkable book of insights may be just 'what the doctor ordered.' Dr. Stephen Guido and Tony Terracciano offer heartfelt, candid insights from their therapeutic relationship — sharing a framework that readers can use to get the most from therapy, helping restore positivity, productivity, and peace of mind."

Michael Brisciana, MBA, SPHR
Author: *A Comprehensive Faculty Development Model*, speaker, and human resources expert

Between the Lines:

Essentials of Cognitive Behavioral Therapy

BETWEEN THE LINES: ESSENTIALS OF COGNITIVE BEHAVIORAL THERAPY

Therapuetic journeys improving interpersonal
boundaries leading to peace of mind

STEPHEN M. GUIDO PHD WITH ANTHONY TERRACCIANO MA

ISBN: 1514174561
ISBN 13: 9781514174562
Library of Congress Control Number: 2015908849
CreateSpace Independent Publishing Platform
North Charleston, South Carolina

To my wife, Phyllis

When I began dating you, I was drawn to your independent spirit. You were focused, loving and totally supportive. I learned then, and continue to learn what is essential in life: the ability to love your family as unconditionally as is humanly possible.

Throughout our journey, you sacrificed a great deal while encouraging me to follow my dreams. So much of the content of Between the Lines *is as much your journey as it is mine.*

You, Phyllis, and our children and grandchildren continue to be an inspiration, and have taught me what is most important: that mutual respect and loving and joyful experiences with each other far outweigh the successes we achieve in life. -- Steve

To my family:

To my wife, Margaret: I want to thank you for being my anchor, and for your continual honesty, commitment and loyalty.

To my children: You have been a source of enrichment in my life.

To my mother, Mary; my father, Benjamin; my brother, Joseph; and my mother-in-law, Marie: Thank you all for always being there for me unconditionally. -- Tony

Acknowledgements

W**E ARE GRATEFUL** for the all of the support we received from family, friends, and colleagues in writing *Between the Lines.* The time, untiring effort, and dedication to this project by our editor, Betsy Salemson, is greatly appreciated. James Browning was invaluable helping to format the book using his computer wizardry, and creating the figures and tables that enrich the content. Stephen Salemson proofread the book for typos and grammatical errors. To Susan Zola, a colleague who suggested that we direct our attention to beginning mental health professionals as well as a general audience, thank you. We enlisted family members to ensure that the content was consistent, and to let us know if they understood unfamiliar psychological terms and concepts. To Michael Brisciana, Anthony Terracciano's nephew, who showed us how we might rearrange the presentation to enhance the main thrust of the book, your suggestions were invaluable. I could never have completed *Between the Lines* without the support, patience, comments, understanding, encouragement, and important contributions of my wife, Phyllis, and our family, Rosemarie Sciales, Ralph and Dina D'Onofrio, and Janine Selgrad. Anthony Terracciano would like to acknowledge the contributions and support of his wife, Margaret, and their children, Linda, Gina, Terry, and Stephen. Special thanks to son, Anthony Terracciano, Jr. and to grandson, 14-year-old Dominick, who share their personal experiences and insights in Appendix II.

This Book is Dedicated to Our Grandchildren:
A heartfelt reminder that the future is yours.

Don't Quit No Matter What!
Edward Guest

When things go wrong, as they sometimes will,
When the road you're trudging seems all uphill,
When funds are low and the debts are high,
And you want to smile but you have to sigh,
When care is pressing you down a bit,
Rest if you must, but don't you quit.
Life is queer with its twists and turns,
As every one of us sometimes learns,
And many a failure turns about,
When he might have won if he'd stuck it out.
Don't give up, though the pace seems slow
You may succeed with another blow.
Often the goal is nearer than
It seems to a faint and faltering man;
Often the struggler has given up
When he might have captured the victor's cup,
And he learned too late, when the night slipped down, How close
he was to the golden crown.
Success is failure turned inside out
The silver tint of the clouds of doubt,
And you never can tell how close you are -
It may be near when it seems afar;
So stick to the fight when you're hardest hit
It's when things seem worst that you mustn't quit.

TABLE OF CONTENTS

Part 1 Becoming A Psychologist: Precursors In My Journey
The Importance Of Boundaries
A Discussion Of Healthy Vs. Unhealthy
Psychological Development

*For those who are conflicted, trapped in life's inconsistencies and
convinced that peace, joy and happiness are illusive*

BETWEEN THE LINES JOURNEYS OF SELF—REFLECTION:
APPROPRIATE INTERPERSONAL BOUNDARIES
AND ATTAINMENT OF PEACE OF MIND

WHEN CREATIVE, INTELLIGENT, compassionate individuals are trapped inside their bodies, robbed of happiness, peace of mind, and the ability to enjoy life, *Between the Lines* will provide the tools to gain mastery of and control over many debilitating symptoms.

Between the Lines is not meant to be used as a self-help book. I have written it to provide an overview and some insight into what is available and necessary for consideration when making the decision to see a therapist. When we are not feeling well, most of us seek expert diagnosis from a physician who may prescribe medication. Likewise, if we are anxious, confused, angry, depressed and feeling immobilized, we need to seek treatment from a psychotherapist. Though medication works well for emotional illness, it is not magic. Many patients have preconceived notions about psychotropic medication and no degree of reassurance and factual information dispels their negativity. There are resistive patients who often sabotage its effectiveness. Also, no psychotropic medication fits all patients and many are not willing to try alternatives within the same category. When medication is appropriate, cognitive behavioral therapy, combined with psychotropic medications, will provide the means to restructure your reactions. Learning the tools of cognitive restructuring in therapy will help you re-establish your equilibrium, improve interpersonal relationships and attain Peace of Mind.

Another distinguishing feature of *Between the Lines* is its emphasis on boundary issues that can interfere with a variety of interpersonal relationships. Part 1 of the book deals with the past six decades and how families are hard-pressed to understand the rapid changes in society and to handle their ramifications and consequences. In Part 2, I, the therapist, invite you, the reader, to experience Tony's treatment during which he was able to access his strong, internal resources so that he could take a leave of absence from teaching and then, using the insights learned in therapy, return to his teaching position after only eight months.

Therapists and non-therapists will recognize the emotional issues that need to be addressed. The personal conflicts described by Tony occurred at a time when cultural, religious and political values were very different from today. In previous decades, sexual mores, definitions of marriage, living together without a marital commitment, same sex marriages, and more, were foreign to him, and to many of us. Many people are still faced with a dilemma when trying to adjust to these changes.

For beginning mental health professionals, the value of the therapeutic interactions provides insights into ways to maintain empathy with patients who are responding ineffectively to conflict. To others who suffer from distorted ways of thinking and consequently experience various mood and anxiety disorders, Tony's experience will, hopefully, encourage you to seek your own therapeutic journey.

The book will underscore the value of psychotherapy and its importance in facilitating the redirection of an individual's quality of life. The reader will understand the universality of the fears linked to our inter-personal relationships: separation and loss, dominance and control vs. passivity and helplessness, phobias, and habit disturbances, to name a few. *Between the Lines* will provide examples of treatment protocols de-veloped for these and other emotional disorders; ways in which to deal with resistive and manipulative patients; and the means for improving today's family dynamics.

In Part 3 of *Between the Lines,* in Chapters 14 and 15, I discuss the impor-tance of techniques like hypnosis, desensitization and dream interpreta-tion in conjunction with cognitive behavioral therapy, provide a more complete self-understanding.

I urge you to peruse Chapter 16, The Author's Reflections, and the Chapter-by-Chapter Summary before you begin reading. You can then be more attentive to the salient points of *Between the Lines.*

Positive thinking will let you do everything better than negative thinking will

-ZIG ZIGLAR

*B*ETWEEN THE LINES was conceived as a helpful tool for anyone interested in examining important features of effective psychotherapy. *Between the Lines* is a metaphor that describes the process of cognitive behavioral therapy (Beck), which involves collaboration between therapist and patient to develop the skills necessary to identify and modify unhelpful behaviors and beliefs.

The term cognitive restructuring describes the building blocks of cognitive behavioral therapy used as incremental steps taken by the patient to help change thoughts and behaviors. I use this skill-building approach to teach patients how to integrate effective problem resolution. Cognitive behavioral therapy does not require an excessive amount of time dealing with past negative experiences. Instead of the more traditional therapeutic approaches, cognitive behavioral therapy provides a springboard to transformation in the present.

Sigmund Freud and a number of his disciples practiced Psychoanalysis and its variations, concentrating predominantly on patients' unconscious and preconscious recollections. The tenets of psychoanalytic therapies implied that talking about emotionally charged events in the past would lead to personality and emotional reconstruction in the present.

As psychologists learned more about the mind, the psyche, and the unconscious, Freudian beliefs were modified. Faced with the devastating consequences of WWII, European psychoanalysts expanded Object Relations Theory. Though psychoanalytic in nature, the theorists focused on the ways in which our psyche develops vis-à-vis others, allowing successful separation and individuation from our mothers. Object Relations Theorist, Melanie Klein, posited that children can only develop object constancy if the mothering they experience is "good enough". This allows the infant to move away from the initial merging toward separation and individuation. (Eagle) Erik Erikson postulated that the mother/child relationship is not only biological but social as well. The development of trust versus mistrust, the first developmental phase in infancy, determines whether future relationships will be built on trust or not, satisfying or unsatisfying, conflict free or not.

The 1970s saw a general cognitive revolution in psychology. Behavior modification and cognitive therapy techniques were merged, giving rise to cognitive behavioral therapy. Cognitive therapy has always included some behavioral components. Advocates of Aaron Beck's approach seek to maintain and establish the integrity of cognitive behavioral therapy as a distinct, clearly standardized form in which the cognitive shift is the key mechanism of change.

Cognitive behavioral therapy uses psychodynamic interpretations, while placing a greater emphasis on altering patients' views of their everyday world. People remain consistent as they learn to modify their reactions to and their understandings of their thoughts, feelings and behaviors. This belief is based on the observation of positive therapeutic outcomes. Cognitive therapists present themselves authentically during therapeutic interactions. Therapists who practice cognitive behavioral therapy do not maintain anonymity but build a therapeutic alliance with their patients.

- Some other forms of therapy are built on the premise that therapists must never share their lives and experiences in therapeutic interactions. I believe, strongly, that this limits us and gets in our way of helping patients confront and conquer their demons. Jeffrey Moussaiff Masson in the chapter Men's Club in *Final Analysis* says:

> We learned, too, that no matter what the question, when it was embarrassing, or one you did not want to answer, the simple device was to throw it back to the patient: "Why do you ask?" Or, a step deeper; "Do you not see the connection with questions you asked as a little girl?" The compliant patient would usually go on to free associate to some event in childhood and the situation would be saved. Above all, we were taught never to reveal anything about ourselves. (104)

> I never accepted the piece of psychoanalytic wisdom that states that every patient gets the analyst he or she deserves. I saw too many cases where kindly, pleasant, affable, and intelligent people linked up, through no fault of their own, with analysts who were cold, remote, unpleasant, and stupid. Other analysts were cruel, even vicious. They, too, had fine patients. The system seemed devised to hide these defects from patients. (105)

- Whereas other therapeutic modalities may require multiple, long-term weekly sessions, cognitive behavioral therapy is relatively short-term and can usually be effective with one session per week.

Cognitive behavioral therapy has become the most effective treatment modality. (Department of Health) The observation that the more psychoanalytic styles of therapy could actually be a hindrance to patients trying to find relief from mental anguish led to the proliferation of cognitive behavioral therapists. Not coincidentally, in the mid-1980s, managed care companies were empowered as the gatekeepers who limited the number of sessions for a given diagnosis.(Horwitz, Allan V.) This monitoring and control of patient care forced mental health providers to look for more efficient and less costly ways to heal patients. As you continue to read *Between the Lines*, you will find numerous examples of the use of cognitive restructuring to improve a patient's quality of life. Cognitive behavioral therapy has proven to have both transformative and practical functions.

I want to restate that *Between the Lines* is not meant to be used as a self-help book. Cognitive behavioral therapy, combined with psychotropic medication, will provide the means to restructure your reactions. Learning the tools of cognitive restructuring in therapy will help you re-establish your equilibrium, improve interpersonal relationships and attain Peace of Mind.

We, the authors of *Between the Lines,* believe that sharing our life experiences and therapeutic journeys will benefit all readers. As you read my interpretations and the insights Tony gained into his functioning, you will understand that therapy is the key to psychological health. The reality of our personal journeys that robbed us of Peace of Mind convinced us to recount our therapeutic experiences and to share the ways in which cognitive behavioral therapy has helped reshape our lives. Recently, during a deeply emotionally painful session, a patient observed, "Mental illness in our society is an issue that is ignored. There is a refusal in this country to focus on it despite its impact on large numbers of people. Many average people suffer daily from emotional stress. We are reacting to real fears, not necessarily to irrational ones."

This has an even greater impact on those who suffer with severe mental illness.

In the first chapter, I describe the precursors to my decision to become a Clinical Psychologist, and the development of my therapeutic style. My personal experiences, prior to pursuing a PhD in Clinical Psychology, were formative in the development of my specific therapeutic technique.

Chapters 2 through 6 concentrate on parenting issues and emphasize the importance of setting boundaries within families. Implications for dysfunctional relationships that result from poor boundary setting are discussed in detail. Many of us have difficulties setting and maintaining appropriate boundaries with other people. *Between the Lines* provides a platform to contemplate the need for setting the boundaries that are necessary in families, with friends and colleagues, and between therapists and patients. If we do not establish boundaries, we are doomed to failure in our interpersonal relationships.

It is of paramount importance to understand the physiology of stress before reading the second half of the book. Chapter 7 helps the reader understand how our brains influence the continuum of stress. As we feel less able to cope, we move from the ordinary stressors of everyday life to the exhaustive stage of stress that culminates in a compete depletion of resources.

Part 2 of *Between the Lines,* the therapeutic interactions between my patient, Tony, and me, reveal Tony's boundary issues with his parents, wife, children, employers, students, friends, and co-workers. Tony is not alone in this. Many of us have difficulties setting and maintaining appropriate boundaries in our interpersonal relationships. (V: Appendix I.A.)

Tony, a patient suffering with real anxiety and fears, presents interpersonal and work related conflicts, while I read *"between the lines"* of the dialogue and share my knowledge with him, Tony shares his pain. My feedback provides interpretations and positive learning experiences. I suggest the origins of his conflicts while offering insights and ways to confront them. The possible conscious, subconscious, and unconscious irrational thoughts or feelings attached to his negative behaviors become clear. Tony uses these insights to develop new behaviors and response patterns. *Between the Lines* is designed to take the mystery and stigma out of psychotherapy.

In Part 3 of the book, I introduce several ancillary techniques that enhance cognitive behavioral therapy. The use of relaxation, desensitization, hypnosis, and dreams, combined with cognitive behavioral therapy, helps patients learn to control their immediate, detrimental reactions to situations and to substitute new, healthier responses. Psychotherapists and other healthcare professionals can coordinate protocols to provide treatment for a variety of emotional difficulties using the same criteria for the diagnosis of mental disorders:

> The American Psychiatric Association's Diagnostic and Statistical Manual Of Mental Disorders (DSM) is a classification of mental disorders with associated criteria designed to facilitate more reliable diagnoses of these disorders ... (p. xli)

> The information is of value to all professionals, including psychiatrists, other physicians, psychologists, social workers, nurses, counselors, forensic and legal specialists, occupational and rehabilitation therapists, and other health professionals. (p. xli)

The criteria identify a range of symptoms from those related to academic or educational problems, occupational problems, housing problems, and other adjustment problems, to the more severe disorders requiring a multi-dimensional treatment protocol.

The point I am trying to make is that all people, regardless of their symptom picture and state of mind, desire to be comfortable in their own lives. I believe that knowledge enhances the likelihood that informed readers will be motivated and afford themselves an opportunity to reflect, to understand and to find peace of mind.

Part 1

Becoming A Psychologist:
Precursors In My Journey
The Importance Of Boundaries
A Discussion Of Healthy Vs.
Unhealthy Psychological Development

1

Becoming a Psychologist
Precursors in My Journey

A journey of a thousand miles begins with one single step

-Lao-Tzu

A PUBLISHER ONCE REMARKED that a reader of nonfiction is not terribly interested in hearing about the author's life. After serious consideration, I made the decision to include a lifetime of personal experience that helped me develop my therapeutic style. I believe that the issues I faced, the therapeutic training I received, and the faculty positions I held at a number of universities all contributed to the development of my therapeutic style.

I have been a practicing clinical psychologist for more than 45 years. My therapeutic training began while earning my MA and PhD. I majored in psychology because of the mental illness I had witnessed in my family. There were six relatives in my mother's family who were severely mentally ill. They had psychotic episodes, visual and auditory hallucinations, delusions of grandeur and persecution, all of which required hospitalization.

Two second cousins were diagnosed with Schizophrenia, and the others were afflicted with Manic-Depressive illness, now called Bipolar Disorder I.

In 1954, when I was 13, I was home with an older cousin. Suddenly, with no apparent cause, my cousin had a psychotic episode. There were no other family members present. My cousin was hallucinating, delusional, and shouting, "There are men in the basement who are waiting for you to leave so that they can attack me."

I was afraid. I did not know how to help. Instinctively, I remained calm. I was reassuring and said that no one was going to harm us. As a result of my calm demeanor and reassurance, my cousin trusted me. Everyone else was suspect. From that day forward, the whole family relied on me, a young adolescent, to provide the calm needed during psychotic episodes. The diagnosis was Paranoid Schizophrenia based on the late adolescent onset of the disease.

This was a misdiagnosis and caused needless suffering. A psychiatrist prescribed very strong antipsychotic medications and Electroconvulsive Therapy (ECT). My cousin suffered for 12 years before I completed my MA and realized that the diagnosis was inaccurate. Though reputable, the psychiatrist had a limited understanding of mood disorders that mimic schizophrenia.

In 1966, I made arrangements for my cousin to be re-evaluated at New York University's Affective Disorders Clinic. The diagnosis was Bipolar Disorder I. Lithium was the drug of choice.

Twelve years of misdiagnoses and failed treatment efforts resulted in physical and psychological damage. My cousin never completed high school, could never hold a job, and had two failed marriages. Lithium was effective but, as a result of ignoring blood level tests, there was a severe loss of kidney function requiring its discontinuation. At age 63, psychotropic medications could only be used sparingly. My cousin remains reclusive and isolated from most of our extended family.

Years ago, my wife and I cared for this cousin in our home to ensure remission each time the symptoms reappeared. During this same period,
I was a caregiver to my mother who also suffered from a mood disorder.
My professional understanding of Bipolar Disorder and other mood disorders underscored what I had lived with. I became my cousin's and my
mother's main source of comfort and support. The never-ending stress
from my mother's psychological illness caused her to develop severe
gastrointestinal problems. She suffered from an ulcerated esophagus
that was diagnosed after exploratory surgery. A manufactured section
replaced the ulcerated section. Witnessing my mother's inability to eat
normally had a profound influence on me as a child.

My mother repeatedly claimed that her inability to swallow solid food
began after I was born. I took this to heart and I felt responsible for her
illness until I was almost 40 when I gained insight in my own therapy. I
remained my mother's dedicated caregiver until she died at 53.

ADDITIONAL INSTANCES FROM MY JOURNEY

While my mother was dying of cancer, I developed serious migraine
headaches. A psychologist diagnosed them as stress-related. A psychiatrist suggested that I get a second opinion from a neurologist. I intuitively felt the migraines were not stress-related. I made an appointment for a
neurological examination but had to wait a month for an appointment.

After my mother's death, my symptoms worsened. I finally was seen by the
neurologist who immediately hospitalized me. I had become aphasic, I was
experiencing coordination problems, and the right side of my body was
somewhat paralyzed. I was 28, married with three children ages 5, 4, and
6 months. I was hospitalized for intensive testing. Within a week of further
tests in the hospital, I could no longer speak and my right side was paralyzed. I had emergency brain surgery to remove an orange-sized, benign
meningioma. The pressure to my parietal-temporal lobe had caused my
symptoms. A stainless steel plate replaces the diseased portion of my skull.

Added to my symptoms was the awareness that I gained in college of my Attention Deficit Disorder (ADD). The effects of the brain tumor and the difficulties that I experienced while regaining my functioning resulted in a deep depression. I consulted a psychologist to help me deal with the inadequacy I felt. The Attention Deficit Disorder (ADD) that I had been dealing with my whole life became more pronounced. My brain could not process too much input. I often panicked when my functioning was impaired.

My brain tumor profoundly influenced my attitudes. I understood then and now that life is precarious. I never assume that all emotional symptoms have purely psychological origins. If there is any possibility of organic roots, I require that patients consult a physician. I caution all beginning therapists whom I supervise to determine if patients' symptoms are psychological, physiological or a combination of both.

In 1980, I began my second therapeutic journey. No one had been able to help me cope with my depression and elevated moods. The psychologist who was treating me provided a great deal of insight. My imbalanced brain chemistry interfered with my ability to use the tools he provided. Two years after discontinuing therapy, I had my first episode of Bipolar Disorder II.

I had been in treatment with two separate therapists for seven years. Seasonal Affective Disorder (SAD) was a part of my symptom picture. SAD causes depression during the autumn and winter. Spring and summer brought relief from my depression. I experienced this pattern throughout my life. I believe this caused the therapists to rely on a purely psychodynamic explanation for my mood fluctuations and to insist that I did not have a chemical imbalance.

After eight months of severe hypomania and a subsequent deep depression, I was prompted by a colleague to seek a psychiatric evaluation. The psychiatrist prescribed psychotropic medication. For the first time I felt relief. I was able to function in a relatively stable manner.

Before I started taking psychotropic medication, I often saw my patients thriving and getting better, while I was haunted by an inability to be proactive in my own life. When the serotonin and other neurotransmitter levels in my brain were high enough to alleviate many of my debilitating symptoms, I experienced a newfound sense of calm and heightened selfesteem. I remember saying to myself: "So this is the way most people experience the world!"

At two different times since then, I decided, without consulting the psychiatrist, to discontinue my medications. In both instances, my debilitating symptoms reappeared within a few months. I now know that I will continue to take psychotropic medications for remainder of my life.

DEVELOPMENT OF MY SPECIFIC THERAPEUTIC STYLE
I have always been aware that people who are caregivers for emotionally ill family members need an avenue to deal with their own stress. Since 2001 there has been a dramatic increase in the number of people suffering from constant stress. Anxiety disorders, particularly panic disorder and Post-Traumatic Stress Disorder (PTSD), have increased since the mid-1990s when school shootings, terrorist bombings and threats, the collapse of the economy, workplace violence, etc., changed the fabric of our society. (Mantel)

From the very beginning of my career, I have been dismayed by the cynicism I encounter among other professionals who feel I work too hard with severely disturbed patients. I intuitively believe otherwise. I maintain my optimism. I try to help even the most disturbed among us achieve some positive emotional improvement. My enthusiasm has never waned. I am convinced that professional cynicism, the result of preconceived, erroneous and failed treatment modalities, is responsible for a patient's lack of progress. Our misdiagnoses, my cousin's and mine, have strengthened my commitment to provide all patients with tools they can use to enhance the quality of their lives.

In addition to my personal therapy, I hired a Diplomate in Clinical Psychology to supervise my treatment of patients. I did this on a weekly basis for 7 years. This ensured that I would maintain objectivity during psychotherapy sessions. I learned the importance of setting boundaries with patients and teaching them the importance of boundary setting in their interpersonal relationships. We mental health professionals have a consistent, ongoing responsibility to sharpen our skills and to remain current.

I have taught in a number of universities, which has helped me remain conversant with new research and treatments for a variety of mental health impairments.

Even in my early training in psychoanalysis, I refused to remain distant and impersonal in therapy sessions. My practice predated modern psychoanalytic thought that has lessened the need for anonymity. I believe in the importance of being highly interactive with patients while maintaining proper boundaries. I understand that treating patients from different cultures, belief systems, and religious affiliations demands knowledge of these differences to prevent me from imposing my values. A therapist must never assess the unusual behavior of someone from another culture as necessarily aberrant. What our Eurocentric culture defines as abnormal may be normal within the context of that other person's society. This concept does not imply condoning the aberrant behavior; it implies the need for non-judgmental yet effective interventions.

In my style of psychotherapy, I am challenging rather than coddling. Reality-oriented psychotherapy, presented by an empathic therapist, allows patients to hear the interpretations and often motivates change. I never tell a patient anything positive unless I believe it is true.

A career in clinical psychology must be taken seriously. Patients imbue us with a great deal of power. They expect an honest exchange based on our knowledge and experience. Making them believe that they are more functional than they are, or minimizing the impact of their negative behavior on others, is shameful. Even delusional patients can learn to accept their delusions of grandeur or persecution as part of their illness, not part of their basic character.

THE AWARENESS OF THE INFLUENCE OF THE THERAPIST

A patient's diagnosis signals the course and intensity of treatment. Diagnoses vary from severe mental illness to transitional, temporary, emotional difficulties. The primary focus of this book is to reinforce the strong belief that people are capable of improving their quality of life. If psychotherapists are sincere in this belief, patients will embrace it. The world is a difficult place filled with stressors that are overwhelming to many people. Good quality psychotherapy focuses on developing coping mechanisms to lessen stress, anxiety, worry, depression, and all of the many symptoms that accompany these conditions. Successful psychotherapy makes a person stronger.

Mental health providers need to re-evaluate the structure of their private practices. We need to provide care without creating economic hardship for families. Workshops designed to educate the general population, support groups, and shortened, less expensive treatment models have increased.

It is important to choose the right psychotherapist. Often the best recommendations come from former patients. As a consumer considering psychotherapy, you have the right to interview therapists to ascertain their effectiveness and training. Too many practitioners in the mental health field avoid examination of their own personalities. This clouds their judgment. You can sense if a therapist appears anxious, ingratiating, and controlling, or is a good listener, is knowledgeable, and is informed about the issues. Many patients I have treated had previously been in therapy with no demonstrable modification in their interpersonal relationships.

There is a place in therapy for increased understanding and resolution of conflict when a therapist examines unfamiliar topics. Suggesting readings, updating the latest research findings and workbooks all enhance self-understanding. Knowing the physiology of stress, its impact on the various organs of the body, self-regulation, and a person's immune system is valuable. Many autoimmune diseases, strokes, heart attacks, gastrointestinal difficulties, sexual performance issues, headaches, back and neck pain, thyroid conditions, and more, may be the byproducts of stress. This understanding motivates patients to modify their lives.

We all have similar fears linked to our interpersonal relationships. We all experience the anxieties of separation and loss, dominance and control vs. passivity and helplessness, phobias, and habit disturbances.

One goal of *Between the Lines* is for beginning therapists to augment their knowledge and for other readers to realize the value of self-exploration and the importance of psychotherapy. Helpful summaries, A Path to Self-Understanding, and appendices are designed to enhance the reader's understanding of negative behaviors. The tools presented can help resolve day-to-day issues and are clarified in the presentation of therapeutic dialogue. In essence, *Between the Lines* has been written for all of us who yearn for other possibilities.

2

Every exit is an entrance somewhere

-TOM STOPPARD

THE FOLLOWING CHAPTERS will cover some of the fears linked to our interpersonal relationships, such as being immobilized by anxiety over separation and loss. The concept of separation anxiety is part of the increasing phenomenon of today's parenting. Many young people are still living at home when their parents feel the burden of parenting should be over. Young adults are living in their parents' homes well into their late twenties, early thirties, and, at times, longer. Even after some have left home to embark on a journey to establish their own families, their paths may lead back home.

Divorce has increased dramatically. In many instances, this sends young adults back to the original nuclear family, and the re-creation of early child-caring roles for the parents of divorced children in crisis. In many homes across America, extended families living under the same roof have become the rule rather than the exception. (U.S. Census Bureau) Parents are experiencing confusion and exasperation over the management of their grown children. These children, on the other hand, are suffering in their own way. They are less able to free themselves of a dependency that is couched in a profound fear of failure and to establish a sense of autonomy and a successful lifestyle.

Chapters 2 through 6 of *Between the Lines* speak to the members of those families who are either currently wrestling with or about to wrestle with the frustrations and confusion of a phenomenon that has gradually become the norm. I hope to provide insight into the underlying dynamics of the modern family. These families are so very different from the experiences of the baby boomers. By providing an understanding of some of the important reasons for the changes in family interactions, today's parents can learn to use the tools they need to help establish appropriate guidelines for their children's growth and independence.

We need to understand certain socio-cultural changes that began in the 1950s and 60s if we wish to view what appear to be drastic changes in family dynamics. I attempt to outline suggestions and ideas that may help parents facilitate their children's journey away from them. In circumstances where leaving may not be a practical solution, I detail suggestions and specific strategies to enable families to live together more harmoniously and productively.

In my professional experience dealing with families in crisis, I have discovered that both parents and their adult children are equally reticent to separate despite protests to the contrary. Separation and individuation are extremely difficult and complex stages of psychosocial development. Through extensive interactions and discussions with members of the different generations, I have identified very strong reactions to and feelings about these phenomena from everyone. In 2012, 36% of young adults ages 18 to 31--the so-called Millennial Generation--were still living in their parents' home. A slow and consistent increase has occurred. The 18-31 age group represented 32% that were living at home prior to the recession in 2007. When 2009 ended, 34% of their counterparts were living at home. (U.S. Census Bureau)

THE HEAD IN THE SAND MENTALITY

There is often a dilemma in many of our interpersonal relationships between acceptance of flawed thinking and denial. There has to be recognition that we must confront the feared reality of uncertainty. Any fear connected to interpersonal loss needs to be addressed in psychotherapy, which fosters a need to move away from the perception of internal weakness and toward the conviction of internal strength. This change in perception ignites pro-activity and planning, an internal shift in feelings and behaviors. So much of our concern about losing a connection with our children, our significant others, and all the people we care about, often creates a state of denial. The denial then leads to a process of enabling. This allows the other person to take advantage of our fear of loss and to use our fear against us. Witness the havoc in homes where the fear of and intimidation by an emotionally and physically abusive family member destroys a family.

Anxiety-ridden thinking is detrimental to problem solving. It is used as an excuse to avoid pain and suffering, to deny the need to deal with the concepts of good versus bad. Denial regarding our fear of loss of another person disguises the wish to avoid confrontation. By hiding from the truth, we suffer with the illusion that we can avoid harm. This encourages failure in reasoning and leads to unwanted outcomes.

We all have experienced a head-in-the-sand mentality. Picture an inverted body placed head first in the sand with legs aimed at the sky.

Preoccupied with the implications and uncertainty of a troubling issue, anxiety escalates. We feel like we are suffocating, spiraling downward like a corkscrew. Our rumination, the sand, constricts and immobilizes us until we reach rock bottom and suffocate.

In many of our interpersonal relationships, we have a difficult time understanding why other people are oblivious to their faults and to their personal contributions to conflicts. We insist that, by pointing out the pitfalls of their thinking, we will provide insight that will change their behaviors. Despite many failed attempts, we keep expecting a different outcome while never once thinking that we are guilty of engaging in similar behavior.

One concept that we must all keep foremost in our thoughts is that we can only control our own behaviors, particularly our own emotional reactions. We all have our own way of thinking, feeling and behaving. Our biases often serve as justifications for our emotional reactions toward others. In chapters 3 through 6, I focus on the need for boundary setting. I have provided a path to self-understanding for your consideration. I hope it provides you with the tools you need to reinforce the learning process.

A Path to Self-Understanding

- Identify an experience where fear led to denial and then ultimately to an unwanted outcome.

- Has there ever been, in your parenting experience, a conflict with setting rules or boundaries with your children? How does the mutual holding onto self-perceptions interfere with conflict resolution? How have you handled such conflict in the past?

3

MILLENNIALS
UNDERSTANDING THE NEED FOR DEVELOPING NEW RULES OF PARENTING

*Your children will become who you are: so be who you want
them to be*

-ANONYMOUS

I WANT TO WRITE about and discuss a phenomenon in our culture that is traceable to the youth movement of the 1960s and 70s. From the beginning of my career as a psychologist in the 1960s, continuing through the 1970s, and the beginning of the 80s, I observed a trend of young adults relying on their parents well into their late twenties and thirties.

My practice focused on family therapy. In their need to keep their children happy, parents encouraged dependency in their children. It is always easier to give in than it is to make tough decisions. The lack of firm boundaries and discipline creates problems. This leads to crises during adolescence. Parents were ill equipped to deal with the adolescent angst that made their children unruly, selfish and impulsive.

When they sought help from me in therapy, I had the daunting task of turning these disaffected adolescents into productive members of society. Suddenly the majority of parents loset sight of their own emotional experiences: confusion over anxiety, depression, self-doubt, sexual identity issues, conflict between sexual desire and parental, moral admonitions, and concerns over the availability of career choices. Sadly, the parents did not understand or accept their own role in helping their children grow and mature. They often chastised me for not changing their children's behavior fast enough.

At the same time, my own parenting skills continually improved. I was able to observe the pitfalls that sabotaged healthy child-rearing practices. Teenagers and young adults have rebelled in every decade. It is not surprising that teenagers go through a period of seeming insanity. The insanity is less harmful when there are clear boundaries and expectations.

Given the complexity of development from adolescence to adulthood, adaptive behavior is needed on the part of the family and the community to further a child's emotional development. All adults need to be mindful of encouraging and reinforcing the creative process unique to each child. All too often, we become anxious when an adolescent thinks differently. It is helpful to remember that all pennies are coins but not all coins are pennies. Understanding the components of creative thinking is obligatory if we want our children to mature into successful adults.

FIVE KEYS TO THE CREATIVE PROCESS

- **Consumption**: The ingesting of experiences and information. Ideas can come in from various sources. The more you consume the more you can creatively draw inferences. New outcomes can become real possibilities.

- **Brainstorming:** The rearrangement of information that you have never previously processed the same way. The evaluation does not imply certainty of a decision, but its potential in the decision making process. Sharing ideas with others to enhance validity of inclusion of the information in decision-making.

- **Critical Thinking:** The evaluation of the strengths and weaknesses of the idea to include the necessary steps to implement the proposal. This evaluation includes the following:

  - What resources do you need to make the idea a reality?
  - What is the most difficult obstacle to overcome to make the idea a reality?
  - What is the worst that can happen if the idea never becomes reality?

- **Incubation:** Do not force an answer. Allow your unconscious, creative mind time to digest and to draw conclusions. It can appear to be spontaneous, but it is your mind's attempt to sort out what is relevant to this new reality. For example, preconceived notions are challenged when you begin to examine them.

- **Production:** Put your ideas into an action that is concrete and representative of your creative thinking. Accept the process of revisiting former ideas to insure accuracy of intention. To insure finality, call it finished and leave it alone. (Handel)

Table 1: <u>This table compares positive and negative parental responses.</u> It is meant to serve as a guide for parents and therapists to familiarize themselves with appropriate and inappropriate exchanges with children to facilitate and <u>reinforce creative thinking</u>

Parental/Adult Input to a Child's Desire			
Positive Input	**Affirmation**	**Negative Input**	**Inhibition**
"I like your idea of bringing your birthday gifts to the children living in the orphanage. It is a wonderful way to celebrate the winter holidays."	*delays gratification for another child's benefit*	"You are going to be disappointed because you will not get the appreciation you are looking for."	*stifles natural instinct of a child's need to be empathetic*
"It's a great idea to include your adult guests in the games at your birthday party."	*strengthens the child's ability to be creative and try new experiences; ensures flexibility and adjustment to change*	"Do not expect your mother and me to organize the adults and still do all of the other preparations. Forget it!"	*interferes with a child's need for affiliation and the widening of a social network; response to a threat becomes a negative motivator inhibiting creativity and autonomy*
"I know you figured out that there is no Santa Claus. You are starting to think for yourself and that's a good thing. However, in keeping with the spirit of the holiday, allow your siblings and friends to figure it out when they are ready."	*encourages the child's ability to think for him/herself and challenge ideas*	"You always seem to have a need to challenge and grow up too fast. You forget that you have siblings. You had better keep your thoughts to yourself."	*inhibits a child's natural instinct to be curious; defeats independent thought and expression*

Note: The inhibitions above frustrate the paradigm Maslow's Hierarchy of Needs (V: chapter 10) in human development.

These are only three examples of adult willingness to encourage or need to control children. Control stifles natural development of the self.

A Direct Application of Communication Skills Fostering Good Parenting Workshop Outline: A Presentation to Parents (April 2014)

Throughout *Between the Lines,* I emphasize that mental health professionals need to provide additional avenues for patients and others to gain insight. Teaching parents how to communicate effectively with their children promotes harmony. Communication skills between parents and children translate to other interpersonal relationships. Effective communication may prevent future family dysfunction and hardship, and destructive marital relationships. Important principles to improve parenting skills:

- Little did I know that the best experience I could bring to the parents who come to listen to me or who consult me privately is that of being a parent myself. My wife and I raised 4 children and we have 12 grandchildren.

- I have a deep understanding of the difficulties encountered in raising and caring for children … the fears, concerns, doubts, and the belief that we need to provide everything we can, and everything our children want.

- What I have learned as a psychologist during the past 45 years is that many of the techniques I use in therapy are applicable to all interpersonal relationships. Cognitive behavioral therapy teaches us the tools we need to accomplish this.

- When I am successful with an adolescent whom I am treating, the parents will often insist that it is because I am with their child for a short time, only one hour per week. Parents want to believe that their children are always on their best behavior when out of the family setting.

- Additionally, parents are convinced that their children have learned to manipulate the environment, their teachers, their friends' parents and, most significantly, me, their therapist, so that we all believe they are problem-free. When people express these kinds of concerns, I begin to reflect on what I am doing. I make the necessary adjustments in my interactions with others. I need to be responsive. I cannot be defensive, argumentative, punitive, harsh, unreasonable, etc. This is important in all inter-actions, and most difficult to achieve within the family.

- By forgetting our humanness, we often make the first error as therapists and parents. The English poet, Alexander Pope, fa-mously told us, "To err is human; to forgive, divine." We must remember that we are real people. We don't have all the answers but we must be willing to work together as a family to solve some of the problems we face.

- The ability to accept a child, or any other person for that matter, depends on a person's capacity to accept. Within the family, one parent is usually more accepting of the children. A great deal, however, depends on the behavior of the individual child. If you think about it honestly, you can probably identify which one of you is more accepting and which of your children is the easiest to accept. I know that I can.

- Please understand, that acceptance is governed by our state of mind or the situation in which we find ourselves. When we feel good about ourselves, we tend to be more accepting of the behav-ior of others. It is also true that we are more accepting of certain behaviors our children exhibit when we are alone with them. We hope that they do not disappoint us when other people such as guests, grandparents, and neighbors, are present

- No parent ever feels accepting of all of a child's behaviors. It is worse to imply acceptance outwardly while seething inwardly with anger, resentment, etc. Children can sense when a parent is insin-cere. We send nonverbal messages of non-acceptance to our chil-dren and to others. These cues, a frown, a lifted eyebrow, a tone of voice, a certain posture, tense facial muscles, are easily read and interpreted. It is more confusing to your children when you pretend to accept them but you do not embrace that acceptance.

- This falseness causes your children to keep testing you to find out what you really mean. And you become annoyed, short-tempered and angry. It is best to admit to yourself and to your children that you don't accept them and their behaviors when they are doing or saying something in a particular manner at a specific time. This will permit your children to learn that you are real, honest and open.

- After all, before they learn from our dishonesty to be defensive, they are open and honest about how they really feel about us. When we are making our children unhappy, they let us know. But this is not always clear to us because we frequently cannot take the time to listen to them and to hear their distress.

- The greatest vehicle for acceptance is to become a listener. When you can feel and communicate genuine acceptance of another person, you possess a capacity for being a powerful helping agent. The acceptance of others as they are is an important factor in perpetuating a relationship in which the other person can:

  - develop
  - make constructive changes
  - learn to resolve problems
  - maintain psychological health
  - become more productive and creative
  - actualize her/his fullest potential

- Simple ... but beautiful paradoxes --
As I indicate in chapter 16, The Author's Reflections, when people feel truly accepted, they are free to move forward and they begin to think:

  - How can I grow?
  - How can I change?
  - How can I become different?
  - How can I achieve my maximum potential?

- Unfortunately, most of us rely on the language of non-acceptance when raising our children. This lack of acceptance poisons the soil of children's development. Rather than blossoming, they are withering as a result of negative evaluations and judgements, criticism, preaching, moralizing, admonitions, commands and demands... all of which interfere with their natural growth and development.

- Some of the ways to communicate acceptance to our children and to others with whom we interact are:

  - non-verbal cues - gestures, postures, facial expressions
  - non-intervention - not interfering with activities; letting the child just be
  - passive listening - in therapy I don't have to say anything to make a patient feel accepted.
  - verbal communication - praising, agreeing, reasoning, sympathizing, consoling, supporting, withdrawing distractions, finding the humor
  - simple door openers - invite children to say more

- Most of the criticism that parents direct at me, the therapist, can be summarized in the one sentence, "You expect us to be therapists, and not parents." My reaction is, if the shoe fits, wear it! I expect you, the parents, to have the capacity to put thoughts and responses in your own words. The truth here is that, when I am home, my wife and children sometimes admonish: "Can you get out of your office head for a minute and talk to us in English?" And it forces me to examine my behavior and to laugh at myself.

- When you use positive reinforcement and listen to your children, you communicate the message that they have the right to express how they feel and that you really want to hear their point of view.

- As you become an active listener, you show that you understand their need to communicate something. You work toward understanding their real communication, the subtext of their verbal message. You can then reflect their feelings by suggesting, "You seem to feel angry, disappointed, afraid", etc. Active listening:

    - fosters the expression of feelings
    - helps children become less afraid of their negative feelings
    - promotes a warm relationship between parents and children
    - facilitates problem solving by the child
    - encourages children to be more willing to listen to parents' thoughts and ideas
    - keeps the problem with the children
    - forces them to think for themselves

- If you want to become an active listener, you must:

    - want to hear what your child has to say, and you must have the time to do so. If you cannot make the time, say so.
    - want to be helpful while listening
    - be able to accept your child's feelings, not impose what you think your child should feel
    - have a deep feeling of trust in your child's ability to handle feelings, to work them through and to find solutions
    - appreciate that feelings are transitory, not permanent
    - see your child as separate from you

- The Venn diagrams, at the ends of chapters 5 and 6 of *Between the Lines,* provide a clear, visual depiction of this concept. Active listening is appropriate when the child owns the problem. It is inappropriate when the problem rightfully belongs to the parent. In chapters 2 through 6, I deal with these boundary issues in our families and our lives.

- If you are having difficulty distinguishing who owns the problem, try using "I" messages. Tell your child how the behavior is affecting you. This effectively places the burden on your child to handle the situation more constructively. If you remain transparently real, if you reveal your humanness, your child will be able to respond in kind. An important lesson to learn is that acknowledging your feelings is not a sign of weakness.

- While you are perfecting this intricate dance with your children, be very careful to avoid venting your anger. Use this emotion sparingly and judiciously. Anger relays a message that makes your child feel blame, guilt, and shame. It is frequently generated by your underlying feelings such as hurt, anxiety, fear or disappointment. Remember, conflict is inevitable in every relationship. Learning what to do with it is important.

- The dyad between parent and child will sometimes result in a power struggle where one party wins and the other loses. Parents have to exercise caution in wielding their strength. When the needs of both parties are at stake, the relationship owns the problem. Conflict is the moment of truth in the relationship and it is a test of the health of that relationship.

- If the parents allow themselves to be manipulated by their children, the relationship between parent and child is compromised. The parents feel they are losing control of their family and they react with knee-jerk, negative responses. This causes the child to feel like a victim, first in relation to the parents and then to society. Healthy cooperation is never the outcome of forcing your child to do something. Frequently, when you think that your child is cooperating, he or she is confused, angry, rebellious, and aggressive. Children in these situations continue to manipulate the adults around them. Our children have more sticking power than we do, and they will outlast us in the struggle.

- When children become adolescents, they are not rebelling against their parents but, rather, against the power their parents hold over them. The more independent they become, the less they are threatened by reward and punishment. Using power as a tool for training children reduces them to the level of animals. It works only if the child is highly motivated to receive some reward. Training is effective with our pets, not with our children.

- In summary, I want to remind you that your children are young human beings. They are just like us. They have feelings. They are intuitive. They sense the dangers of their world. From the moment of their birth, our children start to separate from us. It is our daunting task as parents to allow them to fail as well as to succeed. Our experience doesn't necessarily translate to our children. If we cannot foster their independence and selfreliance, then we have failed as parents.

Table 2: The table below compares unreasonable beliefs and their alternatives. It includes examples of the application of cognitive restructuring in negotiating conflicts. (Robin, Foster)

Common Unreasonable Beliefs and Alternatives

	Unreasonable Belief	Reasonable Alternative
Parents		
Ruination	"If my teenager is given freedom and/or rules are relaxed, catastrophic consequences will result, which will ruin the teenager's future."	"Come on! Many teenagers are given additional freedom without any bad reactions. Am I truly being realistic?"
Obedience	"My teenager should always do what I ask or demand, and it is catastrophic if s/he fails to obey me."	"Did I always listen to my parents? Have I turned out terrible? What is the worst thing that can happen?"
Perfectionism	"My teenager should always know the right thing to do and should always make the right decision."	"Teenagers, like parents, make mistakes and have a right to learn from their mistakes. No one is perfect."
Self-blame	"It is my fault when my teenager acts out or makes mistakes. If only I had raised the child differently, this would never have happened."	"We can only guide our children. We cannot ultimately be responsible for all of their behavior. Many other people have also influenced my teen."
Malicious intent	"My teenager is misbehaving on purpose to annoy, hurt, and anger my spouse and me."	"Teenagers don't generally plan their misbehavior in advance. What are some other explanations for why it appears as if my teen is trying to hurt me?"
Adolescents		
Fairness	"It is terribly unfair for my parents to enforce rules."	"Parents have a right to let me know how they feel. Who promised life will always be fair?"
Ruination	"Parent's rules will ruin my life by stopping me from having a good time, having friends, or doing what other teenagers do."	"When was the last time a parental rule interfered with my plans? Did everything fall apart? Did I lose all my friends? Come on! What is the worst thing that can really happen?"
Autonomy	"I should be permitted total freedom to do whatever I want without any parental interference."	"Does anyone really have such freedom? Don't I really want help sometimes? Parents have a right to guide me, just as I have a right to let them know how I feel. We need to respect each other's rights."
Approval	"It is terrible for me to do things that upset my parents."	"I can't please everyone all the time. I must say what I think, even if my parents don't agree."

There are other significant needs for furthering a child's emotional development. For example, if a child does not appear to demonstrate the academic skills needed to succeed in college, the best interest of the child is better served if the agenda corresponds to the child's interests, aptitudes, and intelligence. Two movies, *Ordinary People* (1980) *and Dead*

Poets Society (1989), are excellent examples of possible dangers of not listening to and/or hearing your child.

A Path to Self-Understanding

- There tend to be two types of motivation that parents use to improve a goal or skill set: negative threat and positive encouragement. Can you separate your child's dreams from your own?

- Perseverance is a necessary trait to overcome obstacles. Suppose your child's known skills are blocked and cause doubt? For example, a Little League hitter works hard prior to the season. Anticipating a productive year at the plate, he experiences a prolonged batting slump. He comments, "I forgot how to hit the ball." The coach challenges the batting slump by threatening a prolonged benching. Likewise, a teacher makes negative comments on a book report aloud, in front of the class. What would be your response?

- When a child has a school project and seeks help from you, how do you balance your need for the child to succeed by completing the project yourself against allowing your child to create the project using age-appropriate skills and abilities?

- Optimism: seeing a glass half-full instead of half-empty needs to be encouraged so that the child does not feel pessimistic and helpless. How could optimism encourage proactivity and avoid unnecessary fear and anxiety?

- Positive emotional development only occurs when the individual has a sense of security. Based on your instincts and perceptions of failed or successful outcomes, what type of environment do you need to provide so that your child feels secure?

- Are you modeling the values that your children will need to help them navigate the turbulent waters of life?

- Problem solving and information gathering can be time consuming. At what point does this expenditure of energy become obsessive and nonproductive?

4

The Origins of Significant Changes: Parenting Styles in the New Millennium

Sometimes we think we're supposed to fix everything, and maybe we're only really supposed to learn from the situation

-Louise Hay

Many parents are probably experiencing a great deal of confusion and exasperation as a result of their children's dependency. If children in their 20s are still living at home, it is hard to identify with their attitudes, feelings and behaviors. If you are in this position, you may wish to leave home yourself.

Nor are young adults in this age group too happy. Many are frightened about going off on their own, and seem to find it difficult to be self-reliant. The years of effort to give them the best for their lives and to be more in tune with their needs backfired. Parents are often incapable of providing the survival tools needed to function in our chaotic world. Children are unable to develop a sense of mastery over their own futures.

Separation, to both parents and children, is a painful struggle, made more difficult because parents do not know how to encourage it. There is no foolproof formula for raising independent, successful children. Although it is the most important job in the world, no one teaches us how to parent.

I believe that many factors in the decades since the tumultuous 1960s have had a profound bearing on our parenting skills, including personality development, inner feelings and temperament, the ways in which we were raised, and the proliferation of media that increases outside pressure for change. The success or failure of parenting is also tied to numerous socio-cultural factors. These influences make it increasingly more difficult for children to deal with issues as they try to move forward.

Prior to the 1960s, age 18 was a magic number. It was the age at which young people were considered adults, and it engendered a certain amount of excitement. There was an enthusiasm about earning adult privileges, alongside a growing anxiety about facing adult responsibility. The rites of passage appeared simpler. Parents, relatives, friends, and neighbors, seemed to agree about societal values. Similar messages were reinforced in schools and houses of worship. The availability of media was limited. Televisions began to appear in all homes in the 1950s, and there was usually only one per household. The family watched the same programs together. It was a seemingly less-complicated time. Common values and experiences eliminated confusion and helped establish a sense of security.

When children reached 18, their parents' job was over. Children had a genuinely good feeling knowing that they were about to embark on their own journey as adults. Older adolescents felt they were reaping the rewards of having survived their own, sometimes dreaded, younger adolescence. The more anxious moments came with the realization of future responsibilities. The draft meant the possibility of going into the armed services. Other choices were college or work. Women's liberation was only an idea, and most young women were generally encouraged to marry. Work was inevitable for those men who chose neither the armed forces nor college. By age 18, many men and women were involved in a committed relationship, and considering marriage. These relationships were expected to culminate in a lifelong commitment to one another.

Sexual attitudes were different. Birth control was not readily available. Fear of pregnancy, strong sexual urges, parental and societal prohibitions, guilt and shame all combined to underscore the virtues of marriage. Children grew up earlier, and parents did not become scapegoats for their kids' choices. The benign neglect of our parents helped us gain mastery over some of the obstacles we faced, but we were not satisfied with the outcomes. This led us to try to raise our children with many more options. In doing so, we raised a generation of self-centered adults who never experienced pain and anxiety. This extreme change in parenting has temporary rewards, and severe pitfalls. Parents in 2015, those who were born in the last quarter of the 20th century, have little history to guide them. They are forging a path while faced with tremendous stressors, and incessant emotional bombardment from a myriad of sources. Their insecurities and self-doubts are transmitted to their children.

Before the second half of the 20th century, 18 year olds understood that they had to leave the comforts of home. When we reflect on our history, the indecisiveness of today's children and their willing dependency on their parents are both confusing and agonizing. Parents are trying to understand their children's confusion and the conflict it provokes. These same parents are unaware of or deny their own issues. Parents have to realize that the struggles they encountered upon entering the adult world were the result of a value system that was somewhat chaotic and removed from that of their children. While good parenting today is the result of many factors that have evolved during the past half century, it is difficult to relearn the ingrained stages of development. Unfortunately, there is no ease of entry into the adult world in the 21st century.

In looking back at the changes that occurred in the tumultuous 1960s and 1970s, I know that, for my wife and me, raising our four children was wrought with anxiety. The identity crisis in young people helped to stimulate a similar crisis in us and other parents. The rebellion and confusion of the time were so frightening that many of us vowed to spare our children similar experiences. Our unmarried peers created a new set of values. We, my wife and I, and other parents found ourselves forging new traditions and experiences with little or no preparation to do so. We hoped to succeed in preventing disillusionment in our children. We believed that love was the solution. In our wish to make the world a better place, we failed to help our children learn how to deal with life, its limitations and disappointments, along with its promise.

Young parents felt a seductive pull to give up the old ways. A splitting occurred in parents as young people challenged society. Traditional values were exchanged for a more hedonistic attitude. Parents unsuccessfully attempted to bridge the gap between the two points of view. The media and advertising did not help. The split was unavoidable.

Parenting was affected by and often resulted in personal struggle. While parents wanted to hold onto the more traditional values, the concepts of family life, hard work, self-sacrifice and delay of instant gratification, they were also intrigued by the idea that their lives might be more enjoyable and personally meaningful. Anxiety grew as parents witnessed increasing numbers of their peers dropping out of mainstream society. Heretofore sacrosanct boundaries were blurred or non-existent. Parents changed their appearance and tried to be their children's friends.

This period of transition spawned many of the ideas that became part of the changing fabric of American values. New, more varied ideas about marriage and the family were beginning to appear. Feminism took root. Women were encouraged to challenge their second-class citizen status. They demanded choices that broke from tradition. Men were encouraged and mandated to share in what were traditionally female responsibilities. Marriage was delayed as more women expressed the desire for careers outside the home. Birth control was readily available. Men and women chose to live together informally.

Parents are trying to understand their children's confusion and the conflict it provokes. These same parents are unaware of or deny their own issues. Parents have to realize that the struggles they encountered upon entering the adult world were the result of a value system that was somewhat chaotic and removed from that of their children. While good parenting today is the result of many factors that have evolved during the past half century, it is difficult to relearn the ingrained stages of development. Unfortunately, there is no ease of entry into the adult world in the 21st century.

Young people were encouraged to delay permanent commitment. Most opted to go to college. They were discouraged from pursuing technology and trade programs, an error that the United States is still paying for. Today, many young people with college degrees find that there are not enough career opportunities available to them. Conversely, there are not nearly enough young people with skills needed in other types of employment. Enter the era of outsourcing.

In order to postpone earning a living, a commitment to another person was out of the question. Prior to this new way of thinking, young adults often left their parents to begin a committed relationship. This mitigated feelings of insecurity, and provided a sense of purpose. Commitment and devotion to a partner strengthened the resolve to make it work. When it appeared that tolerating inconveniences, doing without, and compromising some needs were no longer relevant, parents were questioning what their own lives would have been like had they not married so young. These frustrations, their willingness to do without and to postpone gratification, had been the building blocks of the emotional development and maturity that so many people believed were necessary to succeed. Lacking that part of the struggle young adults could choose to exist on their own terms.

The self-gratification philosophy adopted by the youth of the 1960s and 70s became the mantra of their parents. Parenting changed with some undesirable results. The economic stability we counted on was dramatically altered. The recession of the 1970s followed by double-digit inflation affected the everyday needs of the family. The pressures caused by cost-of-living changes became important. The easy availability of drugs resulted in enormous numbers of people turning to drug-induced numbness to cope with or to avoid the demands of life. These factors contributed to the need to hold onto children. Keeping children home was safer. This trend persists. This symbiotic relationship creates mutual conflict, stress, and an enabling process that is never-ending. Parents today worry about whether or not their children should ever leave.

The 1970s ended with American family life undergoing profound changes. The emphasis on extended education, its higher cost, and the increasing shortage of affordable housing, made staying at home longer more sensible. The rising divorce rate serves as a warning to children to be cautious about choosing a mate. This adds to the trend toward later marriages. These developments compel our children to depend more on us. As resentment seeps in, we forget our contribution to the mess we helped create.

Dating rituals have changed. Technology has overshadowed traditional ways of communicating, and socializing. Privacy issues abound. Many young adults are subject to the harshness of disgruntled friends who reveal intimate communications on social networks. The bar scene has a different meaning than it did during the disco craze of the late 1970s and early 1980s. Our children are frightened about falling victim to AIDS and other STDs. They are concerned about alcohol abuse and the price they would pay if arrested or injured while driving drunk. This latter awareness is laudable and has given rise to the need to practice restraint. Without alcohol to help them relax, it seems to be more difficult for today's young people to date and socialize. Not having the resources to explore alternative ways to meet their peers, today's young adults are floundering. The personal ad, once considered acceptable only to the social outcasts or extreme religious groups, and the more recent profiles on sites that try to match people by commonalities have become popular substitutes.

Without a committed relationship, venturing away from the family is more difficult. Parents ask, "Why haven't you met someone?" Children get defensive. They feel that they should be much further along their life's journey. The similarities between today's conservative leanings, and the feelings and attitudes experienced in the 1940s and 50s have come almost full circle even while incorporating important benefits from the soul-searching of the 1960s and 70s. We embrace the importance of improved communication between spouses and across generations.

We have better ways in which to talk to one another. We are more open. We encourage our children to express their feelings and concerns to us. Greater sexual awareness and being comfortable with personal sexuality, and the emphasis upon parenting being a joint effort for men and women, are all important outgrowths of that time. We recognize that some of the changes made as a result of experiences in self-reflection created uncertainty and confusion that carried over to parenting. The current backlash of a great number of Americans committed to the right to life, condemnations of same sex marriages, and blocking gun legislation makes us question whether the ideas we were raised with were indeed more ingrained than we thought. We need to blend the more traditional values of the mid-20th Century with the realities of the 21st Century. If we succeed, we will be able to promote our children's healthy journey away from home.

As you read the chapters that follow, your fear of letting go and your children's need to hold on will diminish. Instead of asking your children, "Will you ever leave home?" you might ask, "How can we work together so that leaving home occurs less painfully for all of us?" If leaving home is not yet feasible, "How can we live together until the separation is possible?"

A Path to Self-Understanding

- What are your views about the content expressed in this chapter?

- What socio-economic factors have influenced your parenting and how?

- Can you identify those biases you brought with you from your parents?

- Have those biases caused you to reconsider whether your parenting should be different from that of your parents? If so how? If not, why?

5

---

*What is the best way to go beyond self-interest and obsession
with personal demands, needs and disappointments? The answer is: Whatever you do, may it benefit everyone*

-GURUMAYI CHIDVLASANANDA

"Sue and I have decided to take our house back!"

Anecdote 1

HAVING JUST ARRIVED home from vacation, Sue and Bob realized the
need to reclaim their home. The vacation had provided them with
enough distance to realize that their house was no longer theirs. They
had relinquished a great deal of their control to their grown children.
They were no longer able to deal with the frustration of living with their
older children. They had hit the wall.

Bob and Sue came home to a smell of disinfectant that barely masked the odor of beer and half-burned cigarette butts. The sink was stacked with dirty dishes; dirty laundry was scattered throughout the bedrooms and hallway; garbage cans were filled with the remnants of elaborate parties. Negotiating the minefields of debris in their home, Sue and Bob retreated to their bedroom. They had hoped this time it would be different. The kids made numerous promises during a family discussion. Bombarded by the stereo music below and the piercing sounds of their 24-year-old son's guitar in the next room, these parents realized that they no longer had privacy even in their own bedroom. There was no chance of holding onto the lingering afterglow of their vacation.

Bob and Sue knew that this scene resembled so many from the past. They had tried talking to their kids about the importance of respecting the rights and privileges of others. Afraid of alienating their kids, they avoided direct confrontations. The thought of their children being angry with them and possibly leaving home created guilt and anxiety. There was always tension just below the surface. They knew it, they felt it, but they always avoided expressing their outrage. They did not want their kids to view them as raving lunatics. Finally, they no longer worried about these things. Something had to be done to regain the feeling that they were in charge in their home. They accepted the responsibility to help their children become self-reliant.

ANECDOTE 2

Barbara was finishing her makeup. Jack had just left for the office with a smile on his face. The privacy that their house now afforded still seemed novel. It had been many years since they were able to start the day off passionately. After 28 years of marriage, the last of their three children had left home. The past three years helped them readjust their lives. Difficult at first, they found it was not so hard to get used to the freedom and spontaneity of making love in the family room, of having a quiet breakfast together absorbed in each other, and of knowing that, at the end of the day, they could recapture the serenity of the morning.

Suddenly, the doorbell rang. Barbara opened the door and her peaceful feelings vanished. There stood Terry, their oldest daughter; tears streaming down her face, carrying a suitcase, a diaper bag slung over her shoulder, and holding her two year old son's hand. Terry explained that her husband, Dave, needed to find himself. Barbara secretly hoped his search would not take too long. As Barbara let her daughter and grandson in, she realized that she felt overwhelmed. Her feelings were mixed. Barbara felt protective and, simultaneously, anxious. She realized that her life at home was about to change in ways that were out of her control.

The change was immediate. Wanting to lessen her daughter's pain, she unhesitatingly cancelled her private duty nursing appointments. The priority was to help Terry. She convinced herself that she could recoup the lost time and income. The uneasy feeling of the sudden and uncertain changes about to happen in their lives gnawed at her. She wondered how quickly the smile on Jack's face would disappear when he learned that the honeymoon was over.

Terry was moving back into her room, temporarily, and their grandson was to have their son's room that had been empty for several years. No more quiet breakfasts together for Barbara and Jack, sharing a few last intimate moments before going off to work. No more were they to enjoy the freedom to come and go as they pleased. Once again, they would be caretakers.

ANECDOTE 3

Living three hours away from her parents had been ideal for Kathy. Her four-year college experience away from home had helped her become more independent. When she first left home, she viewed her dormitory room and the entire college campus as a refuge. She would be able to make her own decisions. It was her choice to study and attend classes. Other than these obligations, which she readily embraced, Kathy was finally FREE. During the previous several years, Kathy repeatedly told her parents, "Just leave me alone. I know what I'm doing. Don't worry!"

After four years of maturity, education and growth, Kathy has returned to live with her parents until she can manage on her own. The transition has not been easy for Kathy or her parents. While away, Kathy came and went as she pleased. She could have friends over any time, day or night, and entertain in any way she saw fit. No hassles...no arguments... She only had to deal with the feelings of her roommate whose needs were similar. Pat recollects Kathy telling her how tuned into each other she and her roommate were. They had negotiated a whole set of rules about their shared living space, a 12' x 15' room. Now, back in an eightroom house, there does not seem to be enough space for her and her parents. Rather than feeling understood, Pat and Don feel ignored. It is as if the last four years never happened.

Kathy cannot understand why entertaining her friends is an intrusion. She wonders why her parents cannot stay in their own room. It is a simple matter of practicality. More people require larger space. It worked with her college roommate, it should work at home. When Don and Pat hear this kind of talk, they feel a knot in their stomachs. "There's a difference here," they think. "This is our house. It's more than just sharing space." For them it is a question of who created, who maintains, and who owns the space.

Kathy likes to say, "It's our house." Pat and Don know that this means something different for Kathy than it does for them. Kathy's parents may seem angry but their real dilemma concerns their confusion. How do they as parents maintain control of their home without causing Kathy to feel that they are ignoring her needs? Should Don and Pat feel guilty if Kathy expresses resentment? What obligation do they have to their grown child ... and vice versa?

RECAP

The parents in each of these situations share common feelings of frustration, exasperation, and confusion. As they try to confront and cope with the various demands of their older children, they feel disappointment. When they were young, they envisioned a sense of freedom for themselves when their children left home. The hardships they endured while raising their children seemed less burdensome knowing that one day the job would be over. Each couple felt they would still be young enough to reap the rewards of their patience and self-sacrifice, and to enjoy a new phase in their relationship with their grown children. The preceding three anecdotes illustrate how their visions have changed, and their dreams have faded. What was to be a happier and more peaceful stage of life has become extremely stressful. Their patience has turned to intolerance.

Each spouse looks to the other for a solution. How do they discipline an adult son or daughter? How do they reclaim their home? How can they help their son or daughter whose journey away from them is faltering? Differences of opinion between them about raising children are more pronounced at a time when they reasonably expected active parenting to be over. This places a greater strain on the parents' relationship, already weakened by years of frustration and the postponement of pleasure.

The adult couples, the parents, want to enjoy their grown children, and, for short periods, they do. The grown children only seem to respond positively to their parents when they, the grown children, can do whatever they please with no concern for their parents. Unless the parents meet their needs with no *quid pro quo*, the grown children become indignant, self-righteous and put off. When asked to lower the music, to confine their socializing to one room, to help with the cleaning or to be responsible for their own wash, the adult children revert to adolescence.

These young adults believe that their parents have no respect for their plight. The reality is that they lack respect for their parents. They refuse to acknowledge the difficulties their parents weathered as they raised the family and postponed their own gratification. Now the parents and their grown children are trying to renegotiate their relationships. Without respect and understanding from all parties, insurmountable conflicts develop and undermine the family dynamic. At this point, these parents are carrying the added burden of feeling out of control in their own home.

Venn Diagram
Illustration of Unsuccessful Boundary Setting

Figure 1: <u>The result of over-involvement of parents in the child-rearing process.</u> This figure uses a Venn Diagram to illustrate how parenting can get bogged down if we do not learn to set appropriate boundaries for ourselves and our children. As our children develop, they must separate from us. Successful adults make healthy decisions to help themselves. Without this growth, we become helicopter parents who spend too much time hovering around our grown children and not enough time pursuing our own lives.

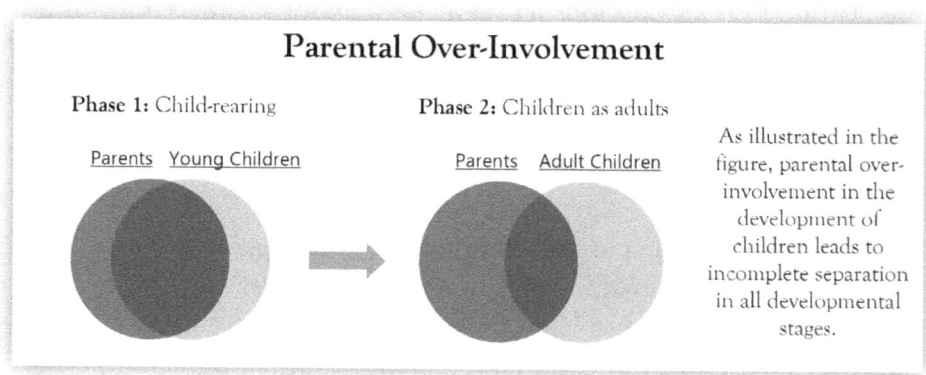

6

You do not need to feel heavy and burdened. There is another way.

-GARY ZUKAV AND LINDA FRANCIS

FOR PARENTS TO regain control of their homes they first have to understand what leads to a loss of control, what outside forces inhibit their decision-making, what their children's feelings and reactions evoke in them, and what influences their feelings and concerns exert on their responses to their children's demands. The discussion of boundary setting in this chapter is not limited to adult children still living at home. It applies to all intimate relationships. Boundaries are necessary for intimacy to thrive and not gradually wither away.

Grown children living back in their childhood home require boundaries. Boundary setting by parents is essential to manage the situation. It eliminates the fear aroused by requests from their grown children who project that their parents are unfair and unfeeling; that their parents' demands show a complete lack of understanding and sensitivity to their plight. Grown children can often induce guilt by insisting there is no appreciation or consideration of their burden while showing no appreciation or consideration of their parents' burden, the continuing years of postponement and delay tolerated during the unending negotiations that led to the present conflicts. Guilt often induces parents to take on their child's feelings. The lack of clear boundaries frequently does not allow parents to separate their feelings from their child's anger, anxiety, or guilt-provoking tactics. Entanglement, created by having few or no boundaries, does not foster parental objectivity. Instead, it creates feelings of desperation and anger for all parties.

Parents have to recognize that our guilt feelings that our children induce are destructive. This is underscored when each parent has different views about what is important. Feeling guilty about earlier parenting decisions often fuels indecisiveness in the present. Grown children may retain their unique way of pitting one parent against the other. One parent may be more comfortable with setting boundaries than the other. If there is no agreement, parents may feel the need to do more, when the real task is to do less. Parents need to realize the real task of parenting: to move children from a state of dependency to that of a fully functioning adult.

Parents need to help their children mature by not satisfying them all the time and by not being the only solution to their children's problems. Children should be allowed to fail. Failure may produce greater determination to succeed. Avoidance of pain can be a motivator for children as they set out on their own journey. The parents in chapter 5 provided more than was necessary and their children were unable to cope with less. None of the children in the anecdotes could tolerate frustration and deprivation. They were unwilling to delay gratification.

Parents need to understand that it is not terrible to expect respect for their feelings. Children need to feel uncomfortable in order to be motivated to want to leave. It is a long-held notion about human behavior that people change when they feel uncomfortable.

In previous decades, it was clear that not satisfying all of a child's needs promoted a healthy striving toward independence. Children continue to be motivated when they accomplish more on their own. This provides a sense of mastery of their world. Success promotes positive self-esteem.

Temper tantrums notwithstanding, proper interventions may initially create disquiet in the house. Parents need to learn to tolerate the rolling of the eyes, the exasperated sighs, and the icy silences of children who do not get their way. These displays of unhappiness by young adults are part of an important growing process that involves pain. Parents often misguidedly rescue children from the pain that will motivate change.

Whenever parents have to let go of their children, they anticipate a feeling of loss. It is a painful feeling. The children feel the pain of loss, too. Nevertheless, that pain can change to self-satisfaction for both children and their parents. Once the child begins to function more successfully in the world, the parents feel a sense of pride as they watch this new independence flourish.

Most of us approach parenthood with some awareness that child rearing is not an easy task. We intuitively anticipate that creating a family is going to present challenges. It is important to build a strong base of mutual respect, and to agree that a healthy supportive family promotes strength in our children who eventually have to make a life of their own.

At first, it may seem impossible for parents to satisfy what appear to be mutually exclusive goals between their children and them. What parents have to determine is, "How can we provide a haven for our children without compromising our need for intimacy, privacy, space and time?"

If parents are confronted with similar scenarios, they need to establish that continuing to stay at home well past 25, or returning home, is only a temporary solution. When faced with the dilemma of wanting to be supportive, parents have to be careful about encouraging childlike dependency. All children, even as adults, unconsciously want to re-unite with a protective parent figure. This scenario rekindles the longing to be one with the family.

An important way of preserving children's adult status is to allow them to attempt to make their way despite the lack of agreement with their choices. Negotiating this critical boundary with more than a suggestion and less of a criticism about the future helps the grown child emerge as an effective adult.

Parents worry privately, and sometimes aloud, about how their children will survive in the current climate. Their hopes and dreams for their child's success can be extremely frightening if parents identify with the turmoil that their child is experiencing. Poor boundaries create a greater sense of fear in the child. Parents project their fears that their children will fail. Children identify with their parents' concerns and projections. This causes confusion and inertia. Parents need to have an explicit dialogue with their adult children. Everyone needs to learn to be less reactive to stress and more proactive in attempts to move forward.

Young adults have the right to make decisions about managing and budgeting their finances, choosing their own forms of entertainment and the hours to engage in them, choosing companions and intimate relationships. It is incumbent on the young adults, if they return home, to respect the boundaries established by their parents. It has to be impressed upon them that it is reasonable to expect their parents to change or realign the rules of the house now that the young adult has returned home while, at the same time, their parents have a right to demand respect in their home. This is the price of returning to the nest.

Boundaries help to further mutual respect among all concerned parties. The returnee has to remember that being at home is a privilege rather than a right. As adults exercising this privilege, they must agree to compromise. They are not entitled to use the house as if it were entirely their own. If young adults choose to go out until four o'clock in the morning, they can't expect their parents to open the door graciously when they forget their keys, or expect their parents and siblings to tiptoe around the house the next morning to ensure their restful night's sleep. With adult status comes adult responsibility. Equally important is the responsibility to help with maintaining order and cleanliness in the house. Young adults need to be responsible for their laundry, dirty dishes, and assorted messes.

The issues surrounding sexual activity ignite conflict. If there is one item that evokes a range of intense and confusing feelings, sex certainly is it. Parents who have younger children in their home have the right to shield their younger children from the older sibling's sexual activities. This kind of behavior needs to be reserved for places outside of the house. Parents have the right to maintain rules that alleviate the confusion that this kind of message would send to the younger, impressionable children. While parents may understand and accept the importance of having a positive and healthy attitude toward sex, this imposed boundary for the sake of their younger children needs to be respected. Freedom of sexual expression requires an appropriate level of maturity and responsibility.

Healthy communications between parents and their adult children includes a dialogue about all of the nuances and realities of sexual activities, which parents cannot realistically control. Parents have to communicate to adult children that, given their age, their decisions are rightfully their own regarding their sexual attitudes and behaviors, as long as those decisions do not interfere with the parents' right to maintain their own value system at home. Parents need to participate in a continued, objective dialogue with their children about sex, especially in light of AIDS and other STDs. They might emphasize the need for promoting a real emotional connection with a partner, but not confusing an intense sexual experience for genuine emotional involvement. This is often helpful in preventing a feeling of disillusionment and disappointment when a sexual encounter is misconstrued as the beginning of a committed relationship.

REVIEW

By now, it should be apparent that, "The house you live in must be yours." If there is still some doubt, then it might be helpful to review what you have read, and to try to incorporate some of the ideas and suggestions I have presented. This may help you strengthen and reaffirm your resolve to take back your house.

There is little doubt that there is a tendency in all parents to try to envision what the future is going to be. Your hopes and dreams reflect, at least in part, your own positive and negative experiences from the past. At times, you hope not to repeat the past; at other times, you would like to hold onto the past for dear life. For those of you raised in a different era, there was no way to anticipate the social and cultural changes that reshaped the contour of your dreams. Some of you dreamed that your turn would come once your children reached their maturity. This so-called coming of age for your children has been delayed or postponed, which has made it more difficult for your dreams to become reality. The result can be feelings of disillusionment and disappointment. You find yourself in the unanticipated quandary of having to continue to deny yourself certain pleasures in order to keep the house going.

You lost your house, perhaps, by trying to provide more for your children than was actually necessary. In doing this, you were partially living out the dream that your kids would have it easier. You may have wanted to shield them from experiencing too much pain or disappointment as they strove to accomplish their goals. You were afraid that too many obstacles would diminish their motivation to work towards accomplishing their objectives. The opposite is probably closer to the truth. You attempted to provide solutions for them that you thought would save them from undue frustration or even failure. In doing this, you were responding to your own needs to protect your children, but were actually standing in their way of experiencing some of the realities of life. Your house became a haven for retreat and avoidance, rather than a safe harbor for emotional refueling.

Their inability to deal with the responsibilities within the house is a reflection of a similar deficiency they have in negotiating the outside world. This inability to act independently and responsibly stems from your need to hold on to them in order to avoid your own pain as you watch them mature. You have attempted to avoid the pain of loss that inevitably comes with any form of separation. Both you and your children are afraid to let go.

The loss of control of the house relates directly to this fear of letting go. Afraid of alienating our children, we are immobilized by our own guilt and anxiety. We question whether we should be imposing our values at a time when they are asserting their entitlement to live on their own. Parents have the right to assert the values with which they are comfortable, and they should. In fact, parents need to spell out what those values are so that clear boundaries can be set. The mistake that parents make is their reluctance to do just that. Because parents anticipate another confrontation that they wish to avoid, they do not clarify their values and standards.

We must also remain cognizant that our older children have reached their maturity and are true adults. If the young adults cannot adequately provide for themselves and still need to be dependent to some degree on us, then it is important for us to find areas in which to compromise. This is a way to provide support for our children, to show that we understand their conflicts. Even though children may believe we set certain boundaries to make them feel infantilized, those lines need to be established to co-exist in some reasonable way. We all want to find ways to convey to our children that we are on their side, but there are certain standards they have to live up to, and certain responsibilities they have to accept. If we can do this successfully, we should be proud of our abilities to live with one another. There is no room here for parental guilt. In fact, we might take a deep breath and exhale a sigh of relief.

A teacher patient related the following anecdote: "When my son was in 10th grade, he failed geometry. He refused help from an outstanding tutor. In college, he said he finally understood that his failure was a result of his dislike for the teacher."

My patient and her husband were high school teachers. Their colleagues could not believe that they allowed their son to fail math. Additionally, my patient, a French teacher, encouraged her son to complete his French requirements a year early. He never took another language class. My patient believed that a high school student was able to determine his own interests and choose his own classes.

When we examine what occurred in this family, we realize that the parents worked with their son to encourage his separation. The boundaries were clear. Though it was difficult to watch him fail, and it was tough to realize that he might never speak French, the family dynamic established the lines necessary for growth and development without guilt or over-involvement. I pointed out that he might never have internalized his right to choose and to accept the consequences of his choices if they had not allowed him to fail.

My patient and her husband were able to guide their son. Because of their mutual respect, these parents convinced him to take two classes he might have skipped or postponed: keyboarding and driver education.

Once again, I want to emphasize the importance of understanding appropriate boundaries and interventions. If we communicate our ideas and concerns to our children, and listen to their responses, it becomes clear how to proceed.

Therapy teaches firm boundary setting. It allows parents to take care of their own needs. It also allows children to experience autonomy throughout their lives. Boundaries permit children and parents to disagree and argue without experiencing loss. Resolution provides the lesson that disagreements are natural and that there are positive results from negotiation. Children learn the importance of dealing with difficulties in the family. When parents model negotiations to resolve conflicts, their children incorporate similar patterns in their future interpersonal relationships. Successful parenting paves the way for the next generation to grow.

I encourage parents to argue in front of children to teach them that it is acceptable for everyone to agree to disagree. Constructive anger is a necessary part of problem solving. It is ok to argue, but with respect. Name calling, screaming and aggressive physical manifestations of anger are unacceptable. If children feel the need to act out, they need a place to calm down in order to have a meaningful discussion. We should encourage children to try to settle their own disputes using the tools they learn at home. When parents intervene, except during physical confrontations, there is a tendency to be arbitrary, particularly if the intervention comes after-the-fact. If it is not possible to determine who is at fault, then both parties are reprimanded to prevent arbitrary decisions. I reiterate that children are very adept at manipulating their parents. It is important to note that boundaries have to be taught as early as preschool and well into adulthood. Trying to set boundaries in adolescence may be too late.

In the interactions between parents and children, the parents must teach appropriate boundaries. Without this, our children will have difficulty with all of their relationships. Children must learn to make choices and to take responsibility for them. Parents need to allow their children to experience the consequences of their actions. This is possible when we incorporate the tools for boundary setting in the family.

VENN DIAGRAM
ILLUSTRATION OF SUCCESSFUL BOUNDARY SETTING

Figure 2: <u>The result of healthy interactions between parents and children in the child-rearing process.</u> This figure uses a Venn Diagram to illustrate how parents can learn to set appropriate boundaries for themselves and their children. As children develop and separate from parents and the nurturance of home, they become autonomous. This growth allows parents to regain their own autonomy and helps all family members to find self-understanding and <u>peace of mind.</u>

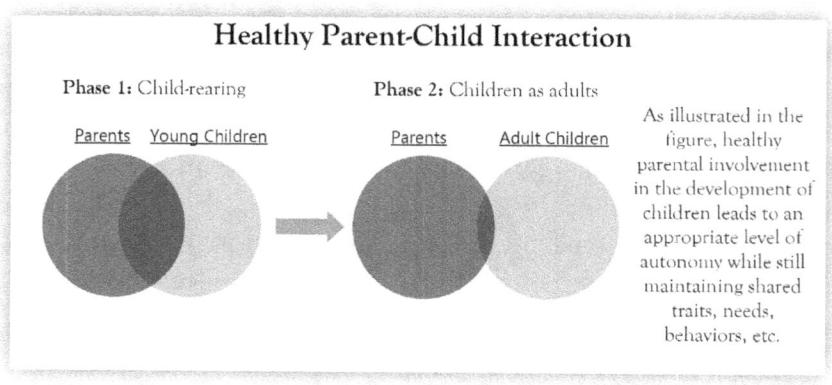

Healthy Parent-Child Interaction

Phase 1: Child-rearing   Phase 2: Children as adults

Parents   Young Children   Parents   Adult Children

As illustrated in the figure, healthy parental involvement in the development of children leads to an appropriate level of autonomy while still maintaining shared traits, needs, behaviors, etc.

A Path to Self-Understanding

- What is your response, whether you are a therapist or not, to what we have presented?

- In what situations do you feel the need to establish boundaries as a therapist, a parent, a young adult, and in other relationships in your life?

- What perceived benefits do boundaries provide?

- What problems can arise without them?

- In trying to set boundaries, what resistance have you encountered, whether your own or from others?

- Can you apply the concept of boundaries to any of the skewed perceptions of those people with whom you interact? What are some of the pitfalls you have encountered?

- In your introspection, what have you decided to do to establish the appropriate boundaries that were not set and are now required to enhance the nature of the relationship?

7

AN UNDERSTANDING OF THE PHYSIOLOGY OF THE BRAIN
EFFECTS OF PROLONGED STRESS ON PERSONALITY FUNCTIONING

Every tomorrow has two handles.
We can take hold of it with the handle of anxiety or the handle
of faith

-HENRY WARD BEECHER

B EFORE ANALYZING TONY'S psychotherapeutic journey in Part 2, a preliminary discussion of the effects of stress in our daily lives will generate a better understanding of the emotional battle within us. We all have a tendency to ascribe our diminished enthusiasm and depression to the uncertainties that await us. Some of these moments are fleeting while others seem to last for uninterrupted expanses of time.

Without detailing the complete physiology of stress, it is sufficient to say that our brain does not make a distinction between the emotion of fear and the symbolic representation of anxiety. Though all parts of the brain and the nervous system are involved in the stress response, for our purposes we will present only one aspect of the physiology of stress.

Fear represents real danger. Anxiety can occur unexpectedly and without apparent cause. Ask anyone who has experienced a panic attack. The endocrine glands and the sympathetic nervous system prepare us to stand and fight, or to flee from the perceived danger. The hormones of the sympathetic and adrenal systems, epinephrine, norepinephrine, and dopamine, enter our bloodstream signaling the need to resolve the conflict. This triggers the limbic system or the emotional brain to get activated. These hormones cause our muscles to contract, while the lungs and heart functions are being stimulated and altered and switched into action.

Through nerve stimulation, the muscles tense, the heart beats faster and harder, respiration quickens and deepens, the pupils dilate and the glands are stimulated to either reduce or increase their secretions, depending on the function of the gland. The adrenals are stimulated and begin dumping out hormones to help answer the emergency signals from the brain. (Robin, Foster)

The source of the fear can come either from the external world or from part of a thought pattern with little or no basis in reality. A panic attack is one response to the increased brain oxygen. Anxiety and panic without intervention develop a life of their own.

Have you ever been in a traffic circle, missed the turn and ended up back in the same place? The physiology of stress resembles this. A feedback loop develops and the worry itself becomes the stressor that causes more anxiety and additional nervous system arousal, which may lead to the exhaustive stage of stress. (V: Amygdala Hijack)

The aforementioned hormones constantly enter the bloodstream and eventually affect all of the major organs of the body. When our body reaches the exhaustive stage of stress, we develop symptoms that include extreme fatigue, depression, anxiety, a sleep disorder, etc.

Anxiety laden thoughts cause the autonomic nervous system to kick in and induce visceral and musculoskeletal reactions. Tension headaches as well as other aches and pains are often the result of prolonged periods of stress. Our muscles are affected. We often experience spasms in the esophagus and the colon, constipation or diarrhea, tightness in the throat or chest, muscle tears and pulls, and much more.

Prolonged stress over extended periods may also affect the immune system. This can lead to rheumatoid arthritis, polymyalgia rheumatica, and fibromyalgia.

- Polymyalgia rheumatica usually only affects the muscles in the hip and shoulders but can also occur alongside temporal arteritis, an inflammation of the blood vessels in the head and neck. Symptoms of polymyalgia rheumatica come on very suddenly and include fever, anemia, weight loss, fatigue, facial pain, malaise, pain in the shoulders and hips, and neck pain. The neck, shoulders and hips may feel stiff as well. (Hughes)

- Fibromyalgia affects muscles, joints and tendons all over the body. It may occur along with lupus or rheumatoid arthritis. Symptoms of fibromyalgia include overall body pain, tender points, fatigue, memory problems, irritable bowel syndrome, tingling, numbness, headaches, and sleep disturbances. (Hughes)

In working with patients over the years, I have observed how stress seriously compromises our body systems. A number of years ago, two cardiologists, Meyer Friedman and Ray Rosenman, noticed a consistent cluster of personality traits in people who were extremely vulnerable to heart disease. They termed this cluster of traits *Type A Personality*. (Girdano, Dusek, Everly)

- An intense sense of time urgency; a tendency to race against the clock. The need to do and obtain more in the shortest possible time

- An aggressive personality that sometimes evolves into hostility; high motivation, yet a very easy loss of temper

- A heightened sense of competitiveness, often coupled with the desire to make a contest out of everything; the inability to play for fun

- An intense achievement motive, yet without properly defined goals

- Polyphasic behaviors: the involvement in several different tasks at the same time

Brain research indicates that the amygdala, located in the midbrain and part of the limbic system, is the storehouse of our emotional experiences. As we mature, a seemingly unrelated event may trigger past traumas. These past emotional experiences may well intensify our present experience exaggerating our immediate response. Goleman (1998) called this automatic response the *amygdala hijack.* (V: Figures 3 & 4)

This amygdala arousal imprints moments of emotionally charged cognitions with an added degree of strength. This explains why we are more likely to remember where we went on our first date, or what we were doing when we heard that the World Trade Center collapsed. The more intense the arousal, the stronger the imprint; experiences that scare or thrill us the most are among our most indelible memories. Our brain has two memory systems, one for ordinary facts and one for emotionally charged ones.

The amygdala hijack helps explain the distinction between two people experiencing similar events. The one who has been hijacked reacts more anxiously. The other person is less reactive, less anxious. A person's arousal system is governed by genetic and learned responses to stress. Figures 3 and 4 show how psychotherapy uses automatic stress responses to help patients identify the original memories and to learn how to control them.

Our brain chemistry may require medication as an adjunct to psychotherapy. We are all vulnerable to prolonged periods of stress. The longer it prevails, the more likely it will cause an alteration in our brain chemistry. Once medication is effective, the tools provided in psychotherapy can be more easily accessed. See following page.

Figure 3: <u>Depicts circular reasoning.</u> It shows how a patient's mind worked when he needed to make a decision. One thought led to another and bounced off to another, as though there were a **pinball machine** in his head. No solution is possible. Anxiety continues to affect reasoning.

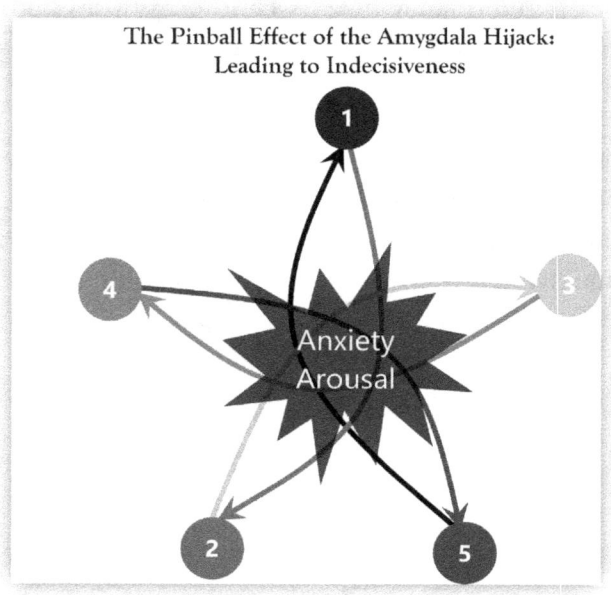

The Pinball Effect of the Amygdala Hijack:
Leading to Indecisiveness

1. A corporate executive, feeling the effects of the economic downturn, began to experience panic attacks that seemed to have come out of nowhere. He entered a state of denial and procrastinated before making an appointment to consult a therapist.

2. This executive's anxiety and depression worsened.

3. He was progressively less able to function at home or at work; which, in turn, increased his anxiety. His cultural background, and his upbringing urging him to pick himself up "by the bootstraps," added to his confusion.

4. After consulting with a physician who referred him to a cardiologist for testing, the panic attacks worsened, in spite of a clean bill of health that gave him a false sense of security, increasing his denial and procrastination.

5. His panic attacks resumed, and the vicious cycle began all over again.

Figure 4: <u>Shows the successful resolution of anxiety.</u>

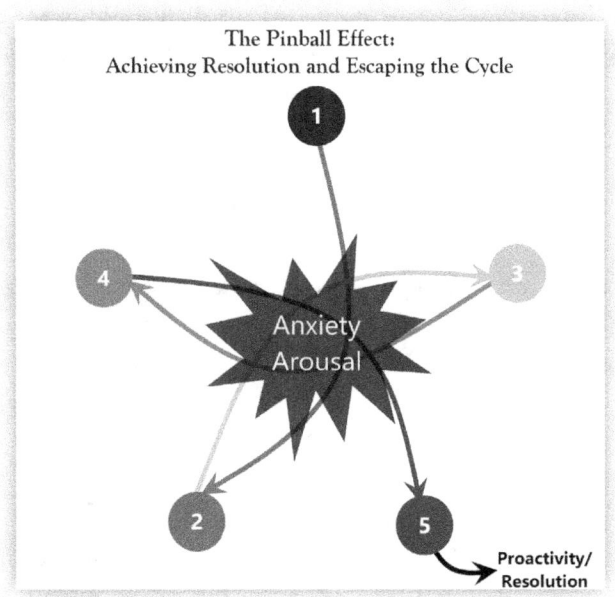

True Awareness: Moving from 1 to 2: A colleague made him aware of his denial. This pushed him to arrange an initial appointment with me, the therapist whom he had been avoiding.

Anticipating Optimism: Moving from 2 to 3: I was able to reassure him by referring to the psychological origins of his anxiety and depression. Optimism gradually replaced the inertia of pessimism.

Trust: Moving from 3 to 4: Our therapeutic connection fostered trust and a willingness to explore lifetime issues that contributed to his exhaustive stage of stress.

Perseverance: Moving from 4 to 5: In the face of adversity, the patient learned to persevere despite wavering thoughts. He and I worked together to develop the cognitive restructuring that allowed him to resume control of his life.

Facing the Demon: Moving beyond 5 and completing the cycle: Controlling the demon: Proactivity and resolution. He made life-changing decisions. His action provided him with hope and renewed his internal resources. He regained his self-esteem.

Acute Stress Disorder

If we are forced, at every hour, to watch or listen to horrible events, this constant stream of ghastly impressions will deprive even the most delicate among us of all respect for humanity

-Cicero

Acute Stress Disorder occurs in reaction to a serious trauma. The symptoms are extremely debilitating. Flashbacks of the traumatic event, anger, depression, sleep disturbances, nightmares, inertia, fear of reentering society, drug and alcohol addiction, sexual promiscuity, and survivor guilt, to name a few, continue unabated if there is no critical stress Intervention. If symptoms continue beyond six months, the diagnosis is Post-Traumatic Stress Disorder.

Identifiable in men who fought wars as long as 3000 years ago, and recognized among our soldiers returning from war in the first half of the 20th century, the DSM-5™ only added PTSD as a psychological diagnosis in 1980. Most people who suffer from PTSD believe that, if they block the memory and never address it, the memory will go away. This is not the case. The trauma remains throughout life, and, later, may cause a severe psychological and/or physiological breakdown.

Anyone who has had experience with war veterans, victims of rape, prolonged domestic abuse, sexual molestation, the loss of a child, car accidents, and other traumatic experiences, knows how close to the surface these intense emotions remain and how easily they can be aroused. Veterans of war, even decades later, cannot speak of their experiences without being overwhelmed. The best anyone can hope for is a lessening of the symptoms over time, but the memory never dissipates.

More About Obsessive Rumination

Our first reactions to stimuli are *in utero*. One example is the positive or negative fetal response to sounds. As the brain continues to develop, it is initially flexible unless there are genetic and environmental anomalies that affect it negatively. The brain is able to process and interpret life experiences and to store them, like a computer hard drive. Genetics, brain chemistry, temperament, and the environment all influence our choices and our emotions.

Various experiences require our attention. The beginning of reasoning occurs in an effort to respond appropriately and to seek closure through resolution. Anticipating, comparing, organizing, qualifying, and judging are all parts of our thought processes. When we are successful using the skills we develop, we can adapt our emotions and our behaviors to our environment. Conversely, we sometimes feel threatened by our environment. Our brain considers the implications of all experiences and seeks to maintain some balance.

Over time, our brain can develop an insatiable need to be convinced, and no amount of reasoning will satisfy its desire for absolute certainty. As thoughts bounce around like a pinball, indecision escalates, immobilization occurs, and the anxiety about making a wrong choice is amplified. Most anxiety is experienced as an altercation within the brain. Inappropriate defensive reactions prevent resolution and closure. The circular nature of the conflict that develops inhibits the sense of satisfaction and finality. Eventually, the previously unencumbered mind is completely overwhelmed, cluttered and out of control.

The next section of the book will help the reader to understand the nuances of therapy. You will learn the significance of the pitfalls that occur and that create negative outcomes. We will discuss the victim mentality in the second section of the book. A victim mentality has its origins in early childhood.

As I mentioned previously, when I was 46, I experienced my first episode of Bipolar Disorder II. I had great difficulty interacting with my patients. Normally, I have a great deal of energy in a therapy session. During this period, I was painfully aware that my patients found my lethargy confusing. It is important to note that the high arousal during a stressful episode adversely affects our cognitive functioning, and we are no longer able to think straight.

South Oaks Hospital, a number of years ago, offered a hospital stay to mental health practitioners who, because of our occupation, became exhausted and *burned out*. The concept of *burnout* is a metaphor for the exhaustive stage of stress. For the general population, *burnout* is a more palatable descriptor than breakdown, which implies mental illness. Had it not been for my wife, the support of my colleagues, and psychotropic medication, I would have needed a recuperative period in the hospital.

Therapists must set boundaries. The boundary between therapist and patient allows the therapist to remain objective. If a therapist begins to take on the emotional reactions of the patient, the therapist becomes overly concerned about the interventions needed to enhance understanding.

Therapeutic interventions sometimes arouse negative emotions in an already emotionally overwrought patient. A therapist with unclear boundaries risks being ineffective in the therapeutic dialogue. Timely and empathic interventions are necessary and instrumental in changing a patient's thoughts, feelings and behaviors, which are the obstacles to maintaining balance and peace of mind.

PART 2

TONY'S STORY
LEARNING COGNITIVE RESTRUCTURING
IN SUCCESSFUL PSYCHOTHERAPY

8

The First Phase of Therapy

Be yourself. Everyone else is already taken

-Oscar Wilde

PSYCHOTHERAPY SEEKS TO relieve us of the negative attitudes that hamper our ability to lead a happy and productive life. Tony experienced forward movement, which in most instances modified or reversed his symptoms of anxiety, and depression. By revealing the nuances of his therapeutic journey, he hopes others can realize the powerful, positive effects of psychotherapy, and the healing it provides. Tony had difficulty separating his own thoughts and feelings from those with whom he interacted.

In the fall of 1993, Tony began his 32nd year of teaching. That summer had been stressful. Financial responsibilities and concern for his family made it impossible for him to benefit from his summer vacation. Normally, by September, Tony was rejuvenated and ready to engage his new students.

Labor Day, September 1993, found Tony mentally, emotionally, and physically exhausted. He could not muster up the energy to prepare for and to teach a geometry course. Though Tony had agreed with the suggestion to teach this course, and had accepted the assignment, for him it was the overwhelming repetition of a negative life-long pattern in which he ignored his instincts when they conflicted with authority. This resulted in his subsequent feelings of inadequacy.

Tony agreed to teach this geometry course to accelerated students as a way to ingratiate himself with the department chair. He was the only math teacher who had not embraced computer science. Concerned with his negative attitude about computer training, he hoped this would distract his supervisor from his, Tony's, avoidance of computer training.

Tony's strong resistance to computer science made it impossible for him to learn it. To fail in the presence of his colleagues was devastating. His increased, uncontrollable anxiety created the feedback loop detailed previously, and interfered with his cognitive functioning. Tony was unable to adapt. His personal demons began to encroach on his professional career. This fueled his sense of inadequacy and his fear of failure.

When the geometry course began, Tony encountered unexpected resistance from several students. Tony's strength was algebra. He was uncomfortable teaching geometric concepts.

Tony had never had difficulty gaining the cooperation and confidence of his students. They willingly learned to follow a routine that made teaching and learning effective. Tony's depressive mood resulted in stacks of ungraded tests and homework assignments.

I believe that this obvious neglect was his students' proof that he did not care about them. This was a new and distressing feeling. Tony's anxiety continued to increase. Tony's teaching slowed and he could see that his students wished they were elsewhere. Tony lost his connection to the class and his confidence gradually and terrifyingly slipped away. The more his inner demons dominated his thinking, the more depressed, anxious, and ineffectual he became.

Tony

By December of 1993, my depression became more pronounced. I was unable to give these students what they needed. I was no longer an accomplished and successful teacher. I developed a sleep disturbance. I could not shut down my mind. My dreams were all nightmares. I would wake up in a panic. I became more and more preoccupied with myself. My family noticed the change. I was quiet and withdrawn instead of my normal outgoing self. I didn't want to leave my home. I felt paralyzed.

I hoped the Christmas break would help me feel better. It was difficult to acknowledge that I needed help. My emotional state frightened me. I felt like I was unraveling. I wanted to hide under the covers and never return to work.

I called in sick the second day of January 1994. I was exhausted. I developed shoulder and neck pains that made it dangerous to drive. My extreme stress began to affect my body. My sudden inability to control my life meant I would never regain self-control. My severe depression manifested itself physiologically, allowing me to avoid my psychological conflicts.

Though I tried to deny it, I needed to find a therapist. I was referred to Dr. Stephen Guido, a skilled psychologist, who immediately helped me understand that I still had the ability to act decisively despite my feelings of depression, anxiety, and inadequacy. Dr. Guido showed me how to counter my negative self-perceptions. I learned to break through my need to short-circuit positive energy. I understood that psychotherapy was going to be healing even though I would have to feel my intense pain. During our many sessions, we examined my personal dilemmas. I was able to internalize the lessons of psychotherapy. I developed a more productive and healthier perspective.

Tony became aware that his mindset served to protect him from previous occurrences. This may have had some practical benefit when he was a child. Using childlike reasoning as adult is inherently flawed. The need to merge with others caused a complete depletion of inner resources. Tony's generalized style of problem solving was overdetermined and obsessive. He has been amazed throughout his therapeutic journey that his severe interpretation of events is often one-sided and not always helpful.

The overdetermined need to understand a given experience, and the belief that obsession leads to resolution and closure actually increase anxiety instead of dissipating it. The anticipated path to resolution becomes the stressor that continues to stimulate the anxiety. It is similar to the folly of pouring lighter fluid on a smoldering wick. The more you obsess about a concern, the more fuel you add to the fire. While it is a simple metaphor, it is the foundation for healing and the first tool to embrace in order to control an obsession. Without this control, the obsession continues to haunt you.

The aforementioned style of thinking, when applied to every anxiety-driven concern, interrupts our quest for peace of mind. A therapist needs to teach this important tool; a patient needs to learn how to extinguish the fire by not feeding it. Obsessive worry is an ineffective, physiologically based stress reaction and learned response that does not quiet the mind. It creates a never-ending, anxiety-driven thought process. We must learn to move beyond our obsessive and habituated form of resolution. At the same time, when used productively, this analytic style of reasoning can be an internal asset.

It is important for mental health professionals to understand that the tools we offer to patients like Tony can be used to modify behavior, to arrest obsessive thoughts, to ensure peace of mind, and to gain control of anxiety, but no amount of therapy will change a person's basic character structure. Psychotherapy provides a path to ownership of and control over our behaviors. It also teaches the need for setting boundaries to increase objectivity.

The positive use of our analytic thinking can reconcile some of the duality, inconsistency, and paradox in our lives, as it has for Tony. I point out to patients that our basic personality is multi-faceted. Long-standing personality traits are so deeply ingrained that we regress to our comfortable obsessive thoughts and stylized negative ways of thinking when we are stressed.

Tony

For most of my life, good physical health was synonymous with overall mental well-being. I viewed ordinary setbacks as weaknesses. I needed to understand that I linked the ideas that conformity, good behavior, and acceptance of authority were the only ways to get approval. Feeling hopeless, I was helpless in face of the ordinary challenges of life. I was no longer able to maintain a balance between my autonomy and my fear of dire consequences.

Tony needed to expand realistic assessments of what was unreasonable and appropriate to ignore. He had always protected himself by avoiding difficult situations. He would store up anger to justify his feelings and his subsequent acting-out behavior. Tony was convinced that his instinct to avoid doing or refusing to do something was fraught with peril. In therapy, it became apparent how this related to Tony's feelings of inadequacy, his energy depletion, and his low self-esteem.

My interventions provided the insight that feeling like a victim for a long period of time is mostly due to the way we interpret our experiences. Learning alternative ways to think about experiences provides us with the tools to gain control of our feelings and reactions, which, in turn, alters our emotional and behavioral responses. As we apply these tools to our lives, we feel less victimized and more self-reliant. This is the process of cognitive behavioral therapy. Becoming aware of and understanding the real meaning of what occurs *between the lines* of our beliefs are important keys to self-understanding. This therapeutic model, unlike previous ones, underscores the crucial need for a well-balanced relationship with the psychotherapist.

The reward for Tony has been to engage in spontaneous decisions, to tolerate ambiguity, and to be more flexible when dealing with stress. This is the positive outcome of cognitive behavioral therapy. It is what we all strive for in our lives.

During the initial crisis, Tony lost the will to experience pleasure. As I do with others who become depressed and anxious, I tried to reawaken the importance of engaging in healthy distractions. Slowly, patients begin to feel better, are more in touch with themselves, and become more animated. Psychotherapy adds further clarity to the restorative energy needed to renew the desire to engage in life.

Tony became motivated. He regained interest in the activities, including music, travel, baseball, hockey, and horse racing, that touched his desire for inner peace; he reconnected with his desires to probe the nuances of thought, emotion, and spirituality. These individual choices afforded Tony a sense of peace and balance. For the first time in his life, Tony was able to take a plane to fulfill his lifelong dream of going to the Kentucky Derby. His desire to be at Churchill Downs was his motivation to conquer his fear of flying. Prior to treatment, he was immobilized by this fear. Until this trip, Tony had never been able to use this convenient way to travel long distances.

Before he returned to teaching in September 1994, Tony proactively requested his previous course schedule, the one he felt was best for him. At the end of August, Tony was ready to return to teaching. My suggestion to be proactive instead of reactive became the consistent tool for most of the anxiety-ridden events that occurred during the course of Tony's therapy. Empowered and in control, Tony realized that life did not have to control him.

I used the concepts of cognitive behavioral therapy to satisfy Tony's need to continue to be thorough, fair, and non-threatening in a way that was more realistic and satisfying for him. By renewing his desire to be enthusiastic about teaching, Tony moved from disillusionment to the insight that reclamation is possible. The coupling of medication with the restructuring of his irrational thoughts promoted a new sense of energy and enthusiasm.

Tony had followed my advice and applied for disability in order to take the time to heal. He accepted this temporary solution until he could get back on his feet. The anxiety about his return to teaching was a major concern since Tony, like many of us, feared the stigma of taking a leave for psychological reasons. His initial, knee-jerk reaction was to conceal the circumstances for his absence from his colleagues. He projected his feelings of shame onto his colleagues who, in reality, were non-judgmental and welcomed his return. He learned that his analytic and metaphoric approach to problem solving kept him well balanced on the one hand, but emotionally handicapped on the other.

Tony

I was able to accept and be open about my emotional setbacks. My feelings of shame and inadequacy became memories. I felt more comfortable in my own skin.

A Path to Self—Understanding

- In what ways has this chapter helped you identify personal conflicts?

- Do you now understand that in order to enjoy the positive qualities of life, an acceptance of an ingrained negative mindset has to be open to change?

- Given an opportunity, how can changing a negative mindset help you to accept and overcome your resistance to change?

- To what extent do you see your state of mind as an outgrowth of past occurrence? Keep in mind the influence of conflict-ridden boundary issues.

- Identify a strong personality trait that you can use to effect change. Why is that trait helpful? The trait could be a tendency to persevere in the face of adversity.

- Are there past circumstances that may have created the strength required for you to access this trait to induce change?

9

---

*The indispensable first step to getting the things you want out
of life is this: decide what you want*

-Bob Stein

I WOULD LIKE TO point out that in Tony's mind there was a constant battle between obsessive rumination and reality-oriented thinking. It is important to get beyond that either-or mentality, to find the grey areas between the blacks and the whites. To accomplish this we need to explore the idea that there is more than one way to approach a particular experience. As Tony began to master this skill, he was pleasantly surprised to uncover a suppressed quality of strength. This underscores the importance of psychotherapy. The process reinforces positive internal strengths that are already present. Psychotherapy provides the tools to rebuild our internal structure. Cognitive behavioral therapy is the infrastructure. As patients learn how to replace and restructure an habitual, historical thought process, they create a new and pristine approach to problem solving. cognitive behavioral therapy opens internal pathways to re-examine our reactions to particular situations.

Tony

As I began to use the tools I had learned, it was easier to understand what Dr. Guido was saying in therapy. I learned how understanding my present reactions could change the ways in which I dealt with my past. He helped me reinterpret past experiences. My anxious anticipation about teaching a new course was related to my need to say, "Yes," when I wanted to say, "No!" This was a repetition compulsion that I needed to overcome.

In my work with patients, unlike some of my colleagues, I often speak about the issues that confronted me during my own life. I was raised in a dysfunctional family with members suffering from mood disorders, substance abuse, and anxiety disorders. Throughout my professional career I have focused on applying the insights gained in training, teaching, supervision, and personal psychotherapy to help the members of my extended family understand and cope with these illnesses. I offered those same insights to Tony as examples of the value of cognitive behavioral restructuring.

When my life experiences were pertinent to his current issues, I drew parallels between the two. I presented these similar, conflict-ridden, emotional experiences in a casual, non-judgmental, manner. I took pains not to be self-serving, but rather to provide an example of someone who had conquered his share of demons and enriched his life despite his emotional struggles and obstacles.

In therapy, I emphasize that patients must embrace the nature of their illness in order to conquer it. There is no room for shame, browbeating, should have, could have, or would have; no reason to allow their symptoms to control, or manipulate others. I warn of the temptation to use their illness, despite the pain they feel, to achieve secondary gain at the expense of others, or to avoid the anxiety that accompanies making the changes necessary to move forward. Tony needed to consider that the disintegration of his internal resources and his subsequent leave of absence, while being of therapeutic value, resulted from his attempt to hide from his confusion, depression, and anxiety. He had become raw, exposed, and completely defenseless. He had reached the exhaustive stage of stress.

How many times have negative memories intruded into our thoughts with the same emotional intensity that we experienced at the time of the event? The questions are:

- Is the emotionally charged nature of the event colored by our sensitivity at the time?

- Does the event dictate the strong emotionally-charged memory?

- Does our original emotional state create the traumatic nature of a relatively benign common experience?

It is my opinion that the answer to each of these three questions is "yes". If an anxious, timid, fearful child, like Tony, perceives an event more intensely because of his vulnerability, the later recollection has a stronger impact that causes an unconscious trigger, which impinges on a realistic perception of the present. Being chastised for seemingly innocent behavior can induce an overdetermined need to become unnecessarily defensive and guilt ridden.

If a map is not accurate, then you cannot reach your destination! Inaccurate conclusions and faulty intellectual reasoning connected with past events impede our forward movement through life. Until we learn to view our experiences more objectively, we are trapped and repeatedly subjected to intrusive false beliefs about others and ourselves. If we are unable to make connections between our thoughts and the emotions they generate, we are unable to transform them into the healthier thoughts and emotions necessary to move forward. In athletics we teach, "No Pain, No Gain."

RECONCILING BOTH SIDES OF THE SAME COIN

Tony's childhood memories surrounding his internal conflict of self-determination vs. his defiance of authority, i.e. rebelliousness at any price, was a consistent theme that continued into adulthood. These issues are common to many people. In Tony's case, there were numerous examples of his need to individuate while, at the same time, feeling stifled. He believed that the consequences imposed by authority figures in his life were not valid, yet he complied at great personal cost. He was determined to avoid the anxiety of interpersonal conflict by trying to find a guaranteed, satisfactory solution to every dilemma.

The uncertainty of our own thoughts, feelings, and behaviors often leads to a what-if mentality, a hyper-vigilance about being judged and feeling pressured to adapt to other people's agendas. Unexpected incidents create the realization that not every behavior can be controlled. This prospect terrified Tony as it does all of us who function similarly. The awareness that outcomes are not always what we intended creates a lack of trust in our intuition and our desires. Vulnerability develops within as we try to cope with experiences that occur from without. We develop an attitude in which we ask:

- "Why engage in an unreliable world?"

- "Why give 100%, only to be disappointed with the results?"

Tony fought these conflicts by rising to the occasion whenever he pushed himself to overcome his resistance. This metaphor is common to many men who experience anxiety about their sexual performance. Many of us develop false energy to accomplish goals that we want to resist but cannot because of an unrelenting conscience resulting from prior experience. We behave like hamsters in activity wheels, expending a great deal of energy but going around in circles. Like Tony, we then develop a victim mentality. We feel offended and misunderstood. Any inconvenience becomes a reason to feel put upon, annoyed, and rebellious. These are all self-defeating behaviors that drain our energy and contribute to obsessive rumination.

This behavior was reflected repeatedly in Tony's alternating moments of first being positively energized, then feeling unsure and inadequate. These cycles were resistant to change and burdened him with a preoccupation about the unexpected. Alternating mood cycles generally suggest a mood disorder. Tony needed a proper medical diagnosis to ensure appropriate treatment. It was possible that a genetically determined mood disorder had been present since early childhood. I requested a consultation with a psychopharmacologist to investigate what medications might help.

To determine if we need psychotropic medication, we all need to consider the following:

- What if the enemy resides in us?

- What if our negative self-perceptions serve to imprison and to immobilize us?

- How do our irrational thought patterns dictate the path of our actions, or determine the social interactions we avoid or embrace every day?

- How do our past experiences influence our present-day behaviors and decisions?

- How does a victim mentality morph into a control Issue? Why?

- What strategies are required by therapists and patients to modify control issues?

The formation of beliefs from our parents, religious community, school, and the media color our perceptions and the resultant decisions; we cannot blame our parents and our past for every failure we experience.

- Can we develop self-defeating behaviors that create our demons on our own?

- Are we willing to accept the unconscious, negative motivations that contribute to our failures?

Tony's numerous impulsive decisions and his penchant to ignore admonitions created trauma that he might have avoided. This underscored his what-if mentality. His genetic make-up and his environment contributed to forces imprinted in his brain as negative experiences. Other children may have similar experiences with less traumatic results.

Tony's earliest memory of confronting authority occurred in Catholic kindergarten. Prior to entering school, Tony's daily interactions were almost exclusively with his immediate family. He was an only child, the first grandson and nephew. Tony was accustomed to being the center of attention. He had little interaction with other adults or children. The adults whom he trusted over-reacted to him both positively and negatively. They were unable to set appropriate boundaries. He was too reliant on their decisions. He never learned to deal effectively with his anxieties.

Tony

The kindergarten program was full day. Lunchtime signaled the end of the morning session. A nun instructed us to get our jackets and coats. I went out of turn. My punishment was to stay behind, alone, in the classroom. I couldn't tolerate it as I had never been alone before. My panic pushed me to get out of there. I grabbed my jacket, ran out of the school with only one thought, "I have to get to my father's Barber Shop."

In therapy, I learned that I was not being disobedient, but reacting to my insecurities and fears. These same ingrained historical, emotional responses cause me to react in the same childlike manner as an adult whenever I feel emotionally disconnected from the people I love. My family's over-protectiveness did not prepare me for the alien world outside my home.

Other children react with less sensitivity than Tony did. They are not unduly influenced by experiences similar to his. (V: Chapter 7, Amygdala Hijack) An individual child's temperament and sensitivity, coupled with negative, harsh parental practices and beliefs, often determine future outcomes. Some children become confused by the special place awarded them in their family. As they develop and grow, the indifference of the real world comes as a shock.

Another frightening and formative memory focusses on Tony's preoccupation with, and anxiety around, illness.

Tony

My pediatrician removed a friend's tonsils and showed them to me just before removing mine. Immediately after seeing the frightening tonsils, I was wheeled to the operating room and anesthetized. My tonsillectomy is a traumatic memory. It exacerbated my feelings that I could not control my life. Others, the people in charge, forced me to submit. If my temperament were less responsive, the emotional impact might not have stayed so vivid in my mind.

Tony recounts a further incident that highlights his long-standing internal war between negative anticipation of outcome vs. the mistrust of fulfilling his desires. This incident also highlights our childlike passion to be in awe of a new experience and our desire to re-experience it.

Tony

At 7, I went to my first Major League baseball game. I can still remember the thrill I felt. I wanted to go back the next day, but my father refused. My aunt convinced him to change his mind. When we got to the ballpark, I did not re-experience the exhilaration and the magic of the day before.

Tony felt disappointed. His father's reaction overshadowed his excitement. This recurred frequently during his childhood. His learned to temper his excitement because of his anxiety about disappointment.

As we discussed his reaction in therapy, I indicated that we all try to duplicate the same passionate, emotional reaction to an event, but frequently there are additional variables. Not only was Tony's desire thwarted, but he felt guilty because he had disappointed his father. Tony's father may have felt the need to counter the lack of boundaries between Tony and his mother. These incidents established the basis for the conflict that Tony experienced as a child and continued to experience as an adult in his interpersonal relationships whenever his wishes were met with resistance.

- Does this mean that Tony had to extinguish the feeling of pleasure from his desires?

- Is pleasure seeking always selfish and overdetermined?

I indicated that we need to be self-serving at times in order to maintain balance in our relationships. I help patients work toward an appropriate balance between caring and empathic behaviors vs. a tendency to be too sacrificial because of a need to be loved and accepted.

- We have to learn that we must achieve a balance if we want to prevent unreasonable and potential harm to ourselves and others.

- To insist on doing what we want to do when we want to do it can lead to compulsive, obnoxious, and impulsive behavior patterns.

These are concerns that all of us must consider in order to create and to maintain satisfying interpersonal relationships. Parents need to understand that giving in to a demanding child or adolescent leads to a number of issues for parent and child. Adults need to develop the boundaries and to establish them with young children.

- When we acquiesce to the demands of a child or another person, it is often due to our need to placate that person because it is less trying and embarrassing to do so.

- The anger that accompanies our capitulation is clearly visible and felt by the other person.

As we mature, we look for validation from others that is similar to the unconditional positive regard we experienced in childhood. (V: Figure 1, Chapter 5) If similar interactions continue to occur, we are not trying to aggravate the caregiver but are seeking an unconditional gift. We, sensing the relationship between the anger and the gift of giving, experience a hollow victory. The unconditional positive regard of initial parenting is not a reality as we mature. This constant seeking of unconditional approval and not receiving it may result in a negative self-image and the distorted belief that the person we love resents being in the relationship.

A Path to Self-Understanding

- Recall instances in your life that have shaped your temperament.

- What are some positive outcomes, strengths, negative consequences, and obsessions/compulsions that result from your temperament?

- We are all multifaceted. Does this insight help you understand yourself? How?

- Ingrained tendencies to consistently respond to stress in a counterproductive way can be modified. How can you access the strengths that are part of your nature?

- Think about the experiences in your past that reinforced your sense of victimization.

- Has feeling like a victim affected your parenting skills?

- Are you inadvertently shaping your child's attitudes and behaviors by re-enacting parenting scenarios similar to those you experienced?

- List the positive and negative attitudes that you may be transferring to your child.

10

More on Cognitive Restructuring
The Contribution of Self-Defeating Behaviors & Failure
Two Sides of the Coin Revisited

The man who makes everything that leads to happiness de-
pends upon himself... has adopted the very best plan for living
happily

-PLATO

A S MENTIONED EARLIER, our state of mind consists of themes that remain fairly constant until we develop insight. Psychotherapy provides
patients with alternate ways of interpreting emotionally-laden experiences.
Cognitive restructuring, learned in cognitive behavioral therapy, allows
patients to understand that their previous perceptions were often self-
defeating, immobilizing, and restrictive in response to conflict.

As Tony continued his psychotherapy, these themes became more
visible, consistently helping him to make connections using newly

formulated insights. In one insightful session, Tony recounted issues that confronted him during three incidents in his childhood and adolescence. These events highlighted the longstanding internal conflict that plagued him; the expectation of negative outcomes as a result of not trusting his instincts when he interacted with people in authority. The following examples accentuate Tony's tendency to be his own worst enemy. I was able to reveal his inner strengths, the other side of the coin, as we reevaluated these incidents. He finally allowed my interventions to make sense to him as he accepted the insights of cognitive restructuring.

Tony

In 8th grade, I got the highest English and math test scores for admission to a prestigious public high school. I chose to remain in Catholic school. I was afraid to leave my comfort zone. I blamed the nuns for my decision when it was my resistance to change, my low self-esteem, and my uncertainty that interfered with my choice.

In 9th grade, I failed the Algebra final exam and, inexplicably, the teacher failed me for the year. I had to go to summer school. I was confused and angry.

Despite a summer school test average of 90, my final grade was 73. I confronted the Principal about the discrepancy. He explained an illogical grading system. No summer school student could get a grade higher than 75. My final grade, 73, did not reflect my real performance. I argued that this should have been stated at the beginning.

I realize that the confrontation and the argument with the principal were the important issues. I challenged his authority. I did not win, but I did succeed in developing a well-constructed argument.

Later, I attended a forum offered about choosing a religious vocation. I asked the speaker how he knew that entering the priesthood had been the right choice. He said that prayer and discernment were key to making his decision. I asked further, "How did you know that you weren't kidding yourself?" The speaker reacted with shock and annoyance. My question was prompted by my need to assert myself, rather than ignore my instincts as I had in the past.

Tony experienced an unnecessary sense of shame whenever he attempted to control outcomes and to challenge authority. Each time he initiated a course of action, his anxiety made him uneasy. He never knew if the result would be success or failure. These experiences increased his inability to make decisions. He had no way to validate his strength in doing so. His choices of travel, his fear of swimming, and his unwillingness to face doctors about physical symptoms created stasis instead of proactivity. His obsessive worry dominated most of his decisions before he gained insight in therapy.

The aforementioned incidents, involving a brush with authority, con-tributed to his victimization, his put-upon mentality. There is no doubt that he frequently placed himself in a position to experience a backlash from authority figures. These instances could have emboldened Tony instead of reducing his self-esteem. His internal strength was there, but he did not recognize it.

There is another piece to this puzzle: risk-taking behavior. Tony often experienced unexpected physical consequences as a result of his behav-ior. It is worthwhile to note Tony's bewilderment and shock each time he was injured, regardless of having been forewarned. His father remarked that Tony learned the hard way. Those of you who are parents may make similar statements to your children. We wish we could protect our chil-dren using our accumulated wisdom, but their insights are learned the same way ours were, through personal trial and error.

How many of us still have a tendency to feel thwarted by the expectations of others regardless of the consequences? Our tendency to refuse to listen can be seen as necessary to our own growth. These situations are part of a war raging inside us. Our desire to challenge ourselves in spite of possible consequences vs. our desire to please our parents or others. Good mental health promotes equanimity, but it requires some thoughtful considerations.

Tony was immobilized when he could not separate his passion from the self-imposed restraints of the other voices in his head. My interventions each time Tony was conflicted about his decision-making freed him to rely on his instincts and beliefs, while not compromising the practicality of his decisions. For the first time in his life, using cognitive restructuring, Tony saw the other side of the coin.

In therapy, Tony learned to recognize his internal strengths, to apply them, and to be realistic about his expectations. This process requires a grounded, centered mindset. We need to trust our own instincts while being aware of possible consequences. If we are willing to endure the personal cost, the consequences may be acceptable. I often reminded Tony that his either-or mentality, his tendency to see things in black and white, did not allow flexibility. I believe that our desires sometimes fall into a gray area requiring an acceptance of outcomes that may not fit our expectations. This does not mean a person has to remain immobilized if there is a possibility of dissatisfaction and disappointment. Using the tools of cognitive restructuring, we can learn from the experience and choose a different approach to reach the sought-after goal.

Another illustration of Tony's willingness to challenge his inner demons occurred when he and a friend decided to ride a rollercoaster. It was a first-time experience. Tony was exhilarated. They got in a car but failed to make sure that the retaining bar was locked. Free falling on the first downhill, they felt as if they were going to be ejected. The joyful antici-pation of riding a rollercoaster was just another disappointment. This incident reinforced Tony's anxiety. Instead of conquering his fear, the fear reinforced his parents' consistent admonitions that spontaneity can be dangerous. Whenever Tony tried to act spontaneously, he heard his parents' warnings. This time he was able to ignore them. He rode the rollercoaster again. He locked himself in. He faced the challenge. He conquered his fear.

One day, when he was 19, Tony went to Pimlico Raceway in Maryland. He did not tell his parents even though he needed to be home by 7:30 p.m. He thought that he could leave the raceway in plenty of time and no one would be the wiser. He expected the return bus schedule to be the same as in New York. He anticipated an exciting afternoon and felt a surge of adrenalin just thinking about the trip. He left New York with $40 in his pocket, a great deal of money in the early 1960s.

Tony

I had been reading the statistics of two horses. When I got to the racetrack, I was encouraged by their positions and I thought they would run well. Unfortunately, I began to listen to other opinions. I bet on the first 4 races hoping to use my win-nings to bet on my two original choices. I lost all four races and was left with only $4.00. I did not bet on either of my original choices. They both went on to win. I had only my return bus ticket, a token for the subway, and 20 cents to make a phone call. I was deflated.

Tony created this scenario. When he realized he had a problem, he did not call home. He began to panic. His family did not know where he was. He was tired, hungry, and emotionally drained. He dreaded having to explain himself. When he got back to New York, Tony had only $.20.

He used it to call home from a public pay phone. He told his family that he and a friend had gone to Pennsylvania and the friend's car broke down. This seemed preferable to admitting what really happened. His mother said, "You mean to tell me that you had no money to call home?" Tony felt stupid and embarrassed.

It is sad that, when we need approval but are fearful of others' reactions, we resort to duplicity. We all know that one lie may lead to another. Tony was old enough to simply state his intent and deal with his parents' objections. Tony continued to deny his wishes to be more autonomous.

I moved on to address Tony's lack of trust in his own judgment as exhibited by listening to the other gamblers. He bet against his informed choices because he was engaged in obsessive thinking. There is never a guaranteed outcome of events. There are too many uncontrollable variables. We all try to make informed decisions but the results are not always what we expect. We are each responsible for our decisions, even when we wish we were not. It is worth repeating that what is most likely to occur when we overanalyze is greater confusion, indecisiveness, and procrastination. The latter prolongs the agony that can best be eliminated by decisive action. It is important to recognize that most choices can be rethought. We have the right to change our mind and to rely on our initial instincts. Forgiving ourselves for our mistakes is a healthy response.

Tony was unable to follow his intuition. The want-what-I-want-whenI-want-it mentality, reinforced throughout his childhood and adolescence, prevailed. We have learned that children who demonstrate the ability to delay gratification are more successful than their impulsive and compulsive peers. Delaying gratification allows people to set long-term goals and to reap greater rewards in the future. (Goleman, 1998) If we do not learn this, our self-esteem suffers. The vacillation that takes place leads to indecisiveness and contributes to the need to act less rationally. We are trapped by the need for instant gratification.

THE OTHER SIDE OF THE COIN:
FURTHER INSIGHTS IN ACCESSING INNER STRENGTH

If we become thoughtful in reviewing our behavior, and internalize the positive outcomes of our more thoughtful decisions, we can learn to master our negative tendencies. As in all situations that create anxiety around decision-making, learning to manage that anxiety eventually leads to mastery. In my experience, selective serotonin uptake inhibitors that temper anxiety allow patients more successful access to the tools learned in cognitive behavioral therapy.

In therapy, Tony identified repetitive, destructive patterns emerging at different stages in his development. The insight came in part from my suggested readings. Following Abraham Maslow's tenets of self-actualization, he recognized that the first 10 years of his life was a time of innocence. Experiencing the world through the eyes of a child tends be idyllic. When left intact and our expectations are met, we are ecstatic. When disappointed, we are deeply hurt and vulnerable. While each of us has to endure the disappointments of childhood, those of us with mood disorders feel the sting more dramatically. We continue to deal with the consequences of our early disappointments throughout life.

Tony

In the late 1990s, the school district chose me to participate in a pilot program to prepare marginally-challenged 9th grade students to take the Algebra Regents, a final the state was requiring for all students. After the first year, I was expected to present my thoughts about the program to school administrators. My anticipatory anxiety was intense.

Tony asked for help with his anxiety. I assured him that some anxiety is natural. It only becomes problematic if we exaggerate the significance of the event. Tony indicated that he believed in the pilot program. I helped him use his passion and enthusiasm to address his audience confidently. Tony integrated his insight to project his confidence as the expert.

Tony

After my presentation, one administrator asked the following question: "How did you address the concerns of marginally-challenged students when learning high level course content?"

From the beginning of the course, Tony used cognitive restructuring with his students. He urged them to embrace the opportunity to learn and to feel the satisfaction of achievement. His enthusiasm and belief in these students served as a model to emulate. Positive and benign dialogue reduced their anxiety, which, in turn, improved their listening and retention skills. As in psychotherapy, a non-judgmental alliance was formed. These marginal students experienced Tony's unconditional positive regard.

Tony

I was asked for an example that would highlight the value of this math program.

I replied using a situation in which two students were able to work together in Portuguese so that the limited English speaker was able to understand the course content. The algebra course was made less difficult by my encouraging this peer learning. This was a positive experience for both students.

We in the math department determined that these students would be more successful if the course were taught over two years. Without the extended time, these students might never have been able to tutor one another. I created an anxiety-free learning atmosphere where students felt comfortable and took chances. They became engaged in their own learning.

What Tony discovered and conveyed was that marginal students could learn more difficult content in a non-threatening atmosphere. The concepts contained in a more advanced course can be taught and internalized. By spending more time concentrating on the sequential steps, the students were able to solve the math problems. The key was the reinforcement of the cognitive skills required to link the steps from the first through the last.

After listening to Tony's presentation, the principal and the department chair encouraged him to become a motivational speaker. When he retired, he remembered their encouraging words and used his talent to motivate others. He went on to teach religious education to interested adults. (V: Appendix II.C.).

Tony learned to take risks by adopting new behaviors without fear. Past events no longer had to shape his behavior and prevent him from acting spontaneously in the present. What he perceived as risk-taking turned out not to be very risky. Even though Tony interpreted his initial life experiences as negative, he learned that they had produced some very positive results: his unconditional acceptance of students, the way he overcame phobias, the manner in which he dealt with habit disturbances such as smoking and overeating, how he managed his health issues, and the ability to mentor his children and grandchildren. (V: Appendix II.A.B.)

READING BETWEEN THE LINES

TWO SIDES OF THE COIN AND THE MANAGEMENT OF STRESS

Table 3: The following table illustrates the benefits of cognitive behavioral therapy for all people. It is a representation of the give-and-take of psycho-therapy. Tony's dialogue with me is in the left hand column. My therapeutic interventions are in the right-hand column.

Resolving Problems Using Cognitive Behavioral Therapy

Negative thoughts, emotions, behaviors	Interventions of cognitive behavioral therapy restructuring
When approaching problems with a black and white mindset...	...find the gray area.
When conflicted...	...think "why not" instead of "what if."
When overburdened with concerns of others...	...understand that boundaries might need to change.
When faced with the compulsion to act because of anxiety...	...tolerate anxiety to overcome the need to act.
When immobilized by a fearful event (e.g., health, career change, relationship issues)...	...be proactive to overcome the "status quo."
When the good you do is unappreciated...	...do good anyway.
When you want to give up...	...regain passion.
When doubtful about making a decision...	...trust your intuition.
When becoming judgmental of others...	...remember your own vulnerabilities.
When tending to be superficial...	...be more authentic and true to yourself.
When you take yourself too seriously...	...find the humor in your actions that are often over-determined.
When pre-occupied with negativity...	...recognize the value of seeking joy and laughter in your life that often goes unnoticed.
When feeling self-critical...	...forgive yourself and recognize your humanity.
When feeling guilty about your behavior...	...remember that guilt can be a motivator to repeat the negative behavior and punish yourself.
When all else fails...	...overcome fear to seek professional help.

11

Distortions, False Belief Patterns, Obsessive /Compulsive Rituals to Protect the Self

A pessimist sees the difficulty in every opportunity; an optimist sees the opportunity in every difficulty

-Sir Winston Churchill

I WANT TO EMPHASIZE, cognitive restructuring means using the building blocks of cognitive behavioral therapy as the incremental steps taken by patients to alter the way they think, behave, and feel. This type of psychotherapy does not require an excessive amount of time spent dealing with past negative experiences. Unlike the more traditional therapeutic approaches, cognitive behavioral therapy provides a springboard to transformation in the present.

Tony's clear and ingrained memories

Below are some additional incidents that led to Tony's continual perceived victimization. These events contributed to his excessive compliant-driven responses to the demands of life while internally he continued to fight for his autonomy. Psychotherapy is both a discrete and continuous process. Earlier therapeutic dialogue about specific traumas and the insight gained inevitably test a patient's consistency in positive resolution of conflict. Tony was at once proud to recognize the previous connections and disappointed when an old response occurred in a new situation. Tony's tendency to flagellate himself was prompted by his guilt at not being perfect.

Tony continued to be preoccupied with the uncertainty about the outcomes of events. This caused him to be overly anxious. To be clear, the event is not what caused his anticipatory anxiety; rather it was the connection made to his earlier life experiences. Tony immediately became energized to complete a task but was immobilized by his embedded memories of disappointment and a preponderance of uncertain results. When Tony internalized the insight that his mistrust of doctors was connected to the trauma of his tonsillectomy, he was able to gain control of his anxiety. But his excessive rumination would inevitably manifest itself during the symptom phase of any new health issue. He continually had to restructure his thinking. In life, fortunately, repetitive opportunities occur for us to practice using our newly gained insights. This helps make it easier to achieve permanency. I refer back to an old adage: Practice makes perfect!

Tony panicked when a hematologist read a chest x-ray and told him about a visible mass. His immediate response was fatalistic. The doctor contributed to Tony's panic by flippantly calling it a "cardiac bundle branch". Tony heard this as a death sentence and made an emergency call to me.

We spent some time considering possible reasons for the results, cognitive restructuring. I offered alternative meanings for the conclusions drawn from viewing the x-ray. I told him that an x-ray is only as good as the technician who develops it or the physician who interprets it. From Tony's description of the area in which the mass was seen, I suggested that it might be an enlarged thyroid. It turned out that I was correct. After seeing another radiologist, Tony learned that jumping into the abyss is often triggered by an unnecessary, confused, and conflicted way of thinking.

Habituated ways of thinking continue in people with chemical imbalances and genetic influences that interfere with their ability to maintain cognitive changes and to adapt to new experiences. Tony often talked about surges of feelings and anxiety reminiscent of his mother's behavior under stress. These feelings were episodic, and bewildering.

We previously referred to the time when Tony needed to be perfect and conform to the department chair's directive to get out of his rut. This left him vulnerable to an excessively anxiety-ridden experience, teaching geometry. He alternated between feeling comfortable, and feeling panicked and frightened. He was unable to battle his demons. The cyclical nature of his moods made it apparent that we needed to address a possible link to a chemical imbalance. Tony consulted a psychopharmacologist who prescribed the selective serotonin reuptake inhibitor, Prozac. He had a tremendous fear of its side effects. Knowing the obsessive component of his personality, I felt the need to work through these fears.

I learned very early in my private practice that the mindset of a patient concerning the recommendation to take medication is crucial to the success or failure of its use. Convincing patients was always difficult prior to 1997 because of the belief that the strong medications given to the institutionalized mental patients were the same as psych meds prescribed to improve the quality of life. It became even more difficult in 1997 when the FDA approved advertising. The severe warnings about side effects from various medications were frightening,

TONY'S FEAR OF TAKING MEDICATION:
AN OBSTACLE TO OVERCOME

I pointed out to Tony that people have a tendency to define the brain in metaphoric terms such as the mind and the psyche. In reality, the brain is an organ and can be dysfunctional like any other organ in the body. Diabetics might have to take insulin; people with essential hypertension might have to take beta-blockers or angiotensin-converting-enzyme (ACE) inhibitors to regulate their blood pressure. Yet, when faced with the prospect of taking a psychotropic medication to help our brains function maximally, we apply a different set of principles.

Tony's thoughts were negative and fear-driven precisely because of his anxiety that the medication would tamper with his mind. In the end, Prozac made it possible for Tony to access his internal resources and cognitions. It changed his mood and behaviors. The medication helped make the tools I provided in treatment more easily accessible. In March 1994, Tony went on disability. By the end of July, he was ready to resume his teaching. Cognitive behavioral therapy combined with psychotropic medication worked successfully in only eight months! (V: Chapter 8)

Some insights that Tony developed during this time were tied to the methods used in teaching mathematics. He realized that he could use these same methods to solve emotional issues.

Tony had explained that math concepts built upon one another in order to reach a solution. He used the term orchestrate as a metaphor for teaching mathematics. Tony understood the algorithmic solutions required in algebra but he had difficulty with the theorems required in geometry. He felt anxious trying to teach advanced geometry students because he was unsure of himself.

When we choose to ignore our instincts, we are disregarding that which we can handle easily. Being compliant with someone else's suggestions to gain approval or to avoid conflict places us in harm's way. Despite our best intentions, we end up with more stress. We become anxious about our ability to succeed. This creates the pinball effect of stress. Tony did not have the emotional wherewithal to teach geometry to advanced students. This task moved him too far from his comfort zone. Once again, Tony created a recipe for failure.

When Tony started therapy, he was convinced that he could no longer teach effectively. Teachers who are 53 years old with 32 years of experience do not frequently leave teaching. Tony was suddenly unable to enjoy the career that had been extremely gratifying.

Successful problem solving in geometry guarantees the only correct solution. By factoring in those elements that could possibly contribute to unexpected outcomes, the correct result is always constant. What is beneficial to geometry students does not work with emotional conflicts. This type of reasoning repeatedly feeds obsessive, conflict-laden, mental exhaustion. The obsessive orchestration of solving mathematical problems interfered with Tony's understanding that trying to control every personal outcome may be doomed to failure. Life is full of uncertainty. We must learn to accept failure as well as success.

It is safe to say that teaching math was the ideal profession for Tony's temperament and for his obsessive need to hide his underlying sense of inadequacy. The positive stressors had previously resulted in positive energy and affirmative emotional feedback. Because Tony focused on his career as the only way of defining himself, his self-worth was predicated on absolute success. Failure diminished him. He became vulnerable. Positive stress became negative stress. Success in teaching was a defining moment. His depression increased because his self-esteem depended on success, and it disappeared with failure.

Tony inevitably became perplexed because his initial success at problem solving waned and he could not duplicate the same determination.

Those of us who eventually come to a more realistic appraisal of ourselves are generally happier. I tell my patients that good self-esteem cannot be defined only by our strengths. It is necessary to accept our weaknesses in order to be comfortable in our skin. Knowing what is too difficult for you to learn is as important as focusing on your talents. Some of us believe, by indoctrination from our subculture or society in general, that all men have an aptitude for mechanical skills. If a man believes his manhood is defined by these skills that he does not have, he will constantly feel inadequate. In addition, men with aesthetic sensibilities who have an interest in art, dance, cultural pursuits or activities like knitting or sewing, question their manhood. In order to have good self-esteem, acceptance depends on a realistic appraisal of who we really are. It is important to learn that no one in our lives or in our culture has the power to define us without our complicit or explicit agreement.

12

---

*Multisensory humans know their goal is not as important as
HOW they accomplish it.*

-Gary Zukov and Linda Francis

IN THIS CHAPTER, we will continue to focus on the other side of the coin, recalling stressful events in which patients are able to use their available internal resources. Most patients do not recognize their strength and courage during conflict and focus only on the negative feelings of the moment. During treatment, I always look for the positive feature that a patient used during conflict resolution. Even in the most emotionally fragile patients, I can find behaviors that validate their strength.

— 101 —

Tony

I was watching the older kids warming up to play stickball. They asked me to fill in for another kid. I was thrilled with the opportunity. I was last in the batting order. We were losing 9-8, bottom of the 9th, two outs, bases loaded, and it was my turn at bat. My anxiety was high. I wanted to prove that I belonged. I concentrated on my base hit earlier in the game. I hit a line drive over the pitcher's head. Two runs scored. We won 10-9. The older kids went wild. I was accepted as a permanent member of the team.

I decided to continue playing. I stayed out past my 8 p.m. curfew. I knew I was in trouble. I did not want to lose my standing with the older guys. I was willing to take a chance. My father was upset with me. He felt that I was inconsiderate and blatantly defiant. The punishment was severe and worse than I anticipated.

In order to understand the importance of cognitive restructuring, in my dialogue with Tony and others, I am both teacher and therapist. I have taught at a number of universities. I keep abreast of the latest developments in psychotherapy and psychotropic medications. I suggest books and articles to read. (V: Bibliography) Reading helps deepen our understanding of the nuances of our experiences. In Tony's case, he learned the reasons why he rapidly moved from ecstasy to agony. He identified his inner strength. I pointed to the negative interpretation he gave to the post-stickball experience. He was able to temper his anxious memory using cognitive restructuring.

Tony learned that several natural needs are part of important developmental processes. By 8, all children are learning by exploring ways to actualize their needs.

I indicated that all of us should keep striving for what Abraham Maslow (Maslow) labeled Self-Actualization. Maslow is well known for delineating the archetypes that we all seek to satisfy our own universal needs. Maslow's *Hierarchy of Needs* explains a great deal about what people require to develop positive self-esteem, a well balanced approach to the unpredictability of life's experiences. The needs in the following table, starting at the bottom, are the most primal. Maslow shows what each of us must integrate to successfully complete each stage. If we achieve Self-actualization, our existence is well balanced and harmonious.

Figure 5: Maslow's *Hierarchy of Needs.*

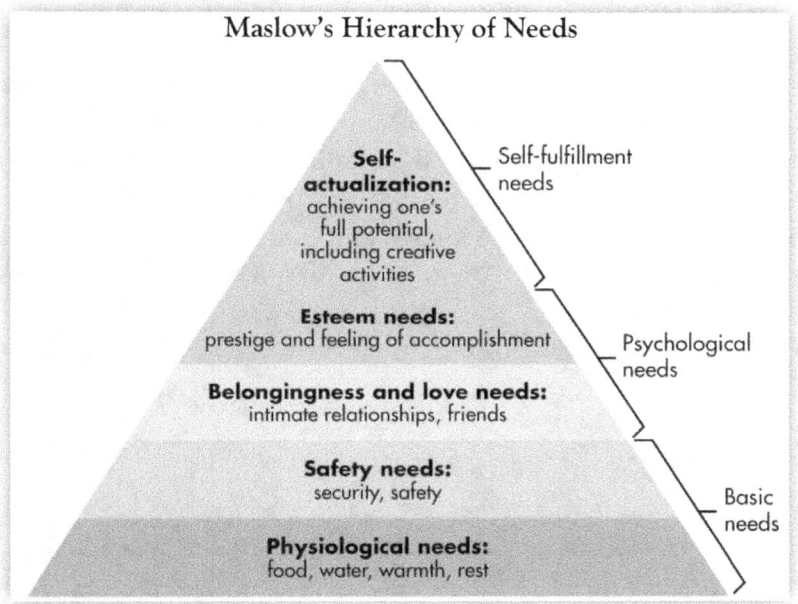

A description of each task that develops over a lifetime is listed below:

> **Self-actualization**: Needs to fulfill potential and have meaningful goals
> **Esteem**: Needs for confidence, sense of worth and competence, self-esteem and the respect for others
> **Attachment and Affiliation**: Needs to belong, to affiliate, to love and be loved
> **Safety**: Needs for security, comfort, tranquility, freedom from fear
> **Biological**: Needs for food, water, oxygen, rest, sexual expression, release from tension

I suggest that patients can use reading material to augment the dialogue in psychotherapy as part of the regimen in which the therapist and the patient must engage in order to:

- Increase the likelihood that the patient will gain insights through the incorporation of reading material in the therapy

- Keep the therapeutic experience dynamic, interesting, and rapid

In my experience, patients enjoy the reading material. It increases their feelings of being an integral part of the process. By being proactive and independent, patients no longer wait for the therapist to heal them miraculously. I enjoy the challenges my profession presents as we work toward resolution of a patient's pain. Tony was an interesting patient whose passion to discover insights created an extremely rewarding therapeutic alliance for both of us.

Tony

After reading about the developmental process of childhood, I was ready to re-script my experiences at my first two major league baseball games and I viewed the stick ball game from a different perspective. I realized that my feelings of guilt, shame, and resentment completely disappeared as a result of our therapeutic dialogue.

I was able to concentrate and hit the ball well. I understood that I could connect to my earlier performance in the game. I recognized my confidence, my achievement, and the status I gained from the group's approval. My parents did not confirm my sense of belonging, or my accomplishment. The physical and emotional pain of the punishment cancelled out the positives and reinforced my confusion. Dr. Guido helped me reconnect with my enthusiasm for baseball.

He pointed out the following things that happened during that 2-hour stickball game, which reflected my healthy development:

- *My love of the game was evident, and I also helped others (Affiliation)*

- *I didn't allow the 11 year olds to intimidate me though I was only 8 (Esteem)*

- *I did not resist, as I was prone to do. I jumped right in (Esteem)*

Understanding the incident with my father did not detract from my experience. Therapy has helped me forgive him and find peace.

Cognitive restructuring allowed Tony to overcome his fear, and to enjoy the sense of belonging, self-esteem, mastery, and goal directedness that the experience afforded. He learned from cognitive behavioral therapy that the positive growth outweighed the cost of the punishment. He might have absorbed these concepts negatively and chosen to become bitter. Instead, he was able to restructure a negative situation to discover what was positive. This was evident to me as he spoke about his parenting, his teaching, his willingness to become a team player and to coach Little League.

TONY'S BRIEF SECOND COURSE OF TREATMENT

After his decision to retire in 2002, Tony discontinued his medication. Without the stress of work and with the lessening of other life stressors, Tony enjoyed the freedom of retirement. His life was comfortable. He and his wife moved to Florida. Tony was still in denial about pursuing what caused his enlarged thyroid. Recall that during the first phase of treatment, Tony panicked when a hematologist read an x-ray of his chest and informed him of a visible mass. His immediate response was fatalistic.

In reviewing Tony's lifetime experiences, it became obvious to me, once again, that though he was often successful in his quest to overcome adversity, he inevitably became perplexed when the success waned and he could not duplicate the same determination. In between Tony's first phase of therapy and his return 15 years later, Tony again lost the ability to access some of his insights and behavioral changes. The reasons for this were twofold: 1) Tony decided to discontinue the antidepressant medication and 2) once he retired in 1998, he was in control of his stress. Then new stressors began to exert emotional tension, and without the stability of medication, Tony began to show signs of emotional trauma.

Tony and the Amygdala Hijack

Figure 6: Tony's anxiety concerning a follow-up examination of his enlarged thyroid.

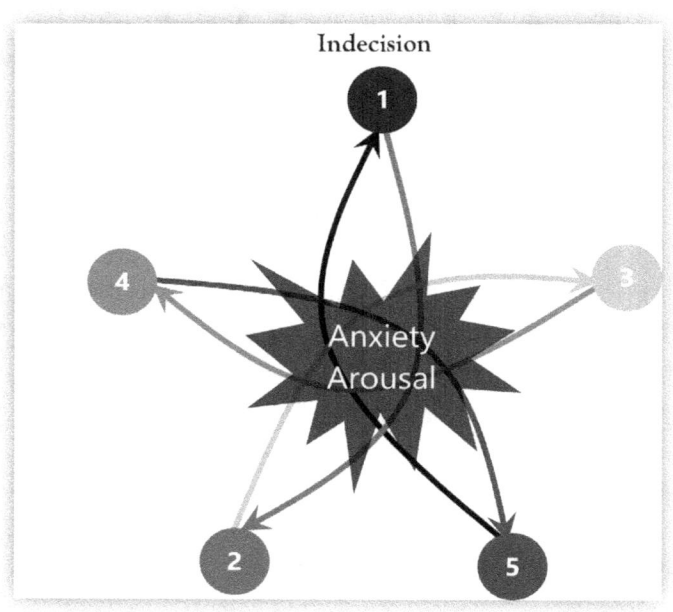

1 Tony, before his second course of therapy, went into a state of denial as he faced a medical crisis. He was supposed to make a follow-up appointment after the initial diagnosis of an enlarged thyroid. Feeling good before moving to Florida, he decided to ignore the recommendation from the New York physician.

2 In Florida, his wife reminded him that he needed to find a physician for a complete physical. Intense anxiety-arousal created concern and the conviction that he would receive bad news.

3 In the recesses of his mind, Tony knew that he had to see a physician. He became more anxious since his confidence about choosing the right physician was poor. What if he chose the wrong physician?

4 After seeing the first physician who referred him for testing, Tony's anxiety intensified because of confusion about diagnoses. A second doctor referred Tony to a thoracic surgeon for a third opinion.

5 Because of Tony's extreme anxiety about surgery, he developed a false sense of security using the confusing opinions as an excuse to avoid confronting the seriousness of his medical issue.

Figure 7: Shows the successful resolution of Tony's anxiety about his follow-up examination. See following page.

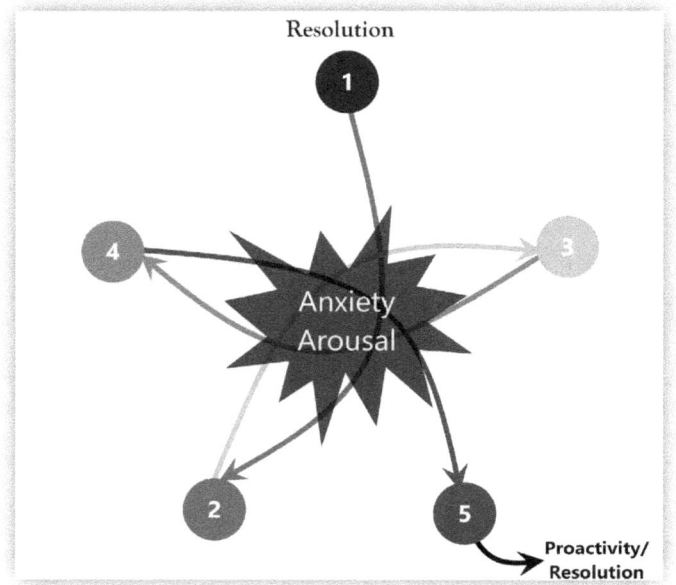

True Awareness: Moving from 1 to 2: Becoming consciously aware of the implications governing denial.

Anticipating Optimism: Moving from 2 to 3: Allowing optimism to replace the inertia of pessimism.

Trust: Moving from 3 to 4: Resolving trust issues. Seeking second and third opinions.

Perseverance: Moving from 4 to 5: Persevering despite wavering thoughts.

Facing the Demon: Moving beyond 5 and completing the cycle: Controlling the demons. Acting proactively to find resolution.

REVISITING BOUNDARIES

In the second course of psychotherapy, I restated the value of affirmative and constructive dialogue in parenting. Tony learned to set appropriate boundaries within the family. He understood that a parent's agenda might not take into account the real interests and talents of a child. The insights Tony internalized have been instrumental in cementing his relationship with his grandson, Dominick, with whom he shares an affinity for baseball. (V: Appendix II.A.)

Tony has called on his passion and experience in baseball during his adolescence to reinforce Dominick's passion and ability. Tony and Dominick have formed a strong bond and alliance. Tony helped Dominick overcome his self-doubt. His belief in his grandson translates into Dominick becoming more self-confident. Dominick learned the significance of working hard, the importance of teamwork, and the use and acceptance of constructive criticism to access his already present inner drive and determination. I can safely say that if Tony's parents had recognized Tony's strengths, more positive outcomes would have been possible.

Tony's father's extreme responses, coupled with the unbendable rules of Catholic grammar and high schools, created intense emotional pain. Tony was self-absorbed and defensive. These tendencies tapped into Tony's narcissism and became overdetermined. His inner rage and confusion about indulging his own desires to enjoy life persisted into adulthood. The need to please others by acceding to their demands always accompanied Tony's search for autonomy. He experienced physical pain alongside the emotional pain of feeling unworthy.

Disappointment fuels negative self-appraisal. This negative introject may imply that such transgressions are sinful. One of the earmarks of Obsessive-Compulsive Disorder is the anxiety-ridden need to do everything right despite the emotional cost. This is obvious when we listen to family members recount myriad situations involving their loved ones with OCD.

I want to emphasize that a genetic predisposition does not definitively predict an ultimate manifestation. There is enough scientific research to understand that some changes in behavior can modify outcomes despite the presence of a genetic predisposition. The son or daughter of an alcoholic may learn to be cautious about drinking and to prevent addiction. There are numerous examples of physical or emotional illnesses that do not occur in the next generation attributable to accumulated knowledge and understanding.

In family discussions surrounding genetic and environmental issues, parents need to find ways to present positive alternatives and to stay away from negative admonitions. I cannot emphasize strongly enough that boundaries between parents and children need to be clear. This prevents parents from bringing their own past, unresolved issues and behaviors into the mix.

Cognitive restructuring teaches positive ways to channel our negative, destructive impulses. Replacing angry responses by turning that anger into assertiveness leads to success. If, for example, we learn to focus our attention, it becomes possible to use an Attention Deficit Disorder to our benefit. Cognitive behavioral therapy teaches us to accept ourselves and to change our actions and reactions. When we achieve this, we are more able to accept others.

Parents automatically serve as role models. We must not allow our recollections of negative parental actions to be our excuse for adopting similar behaviors with our own children. This was the case with his father's anger when Tony chose to play stickball and to ignore his curfew.

Tony's father, Benjamin, was born in 1915 and grew up during the Great Depression. His own father, Tony's paternal grandfather, left Italy for America in search of a more productive life. Tony's paternal grandmother died when Benjamin, her son, was 4 years old. He remembered hearing her beseech his aunt, "Please take care of him (Benjamin)." As an adult, Benjamin owned a successful business. In the 1920s and 30s, parents subscribed to the philosophy, "Spare the rod and spoil the child." Benjamin believed that strict parenting would help his children. An unfortunate corollary of that belief is the unwillingness to express feelings, which are viewed as weaknesses. Tony's father belonged to a generation that did not tolerate failure among their children. They did not realize that positive, emotive reinforcement creates happy, successful adults.

Benjamin's expectations were unrealistic. He wanted his son, Tony, to conform to his, Benjamin's, way. This created a sense of emotional imbalance that contributed to Tony's hyper-vigilance about the unpredictably of life. Tony was confused and anxious when he had to make decisions. He flagellated himself for not anticipating the right behaviors. He tended to be inordinately sensitive and defensive across a broad spectrum of occurrences. His constant worry fueled his obsessive rumination about unpredictable outcomes.

Sometimes, when our parental models are not reliable for teaching survival skills, we attach ourselves to another adult and we place unreasonable expectations on that person. Our vulnerability causes us to be less discerning, and we are disappointed. Mentors can be extremely helpful, but when we invest all of our dependency needs in them, we become less self-reliant. Mentors can have clay feet. It is important to establish boundaries here, in this relationship, too. We have to work at maintaining our independence of thought and relying on our intuition. We need to be open to alternative solutions and approaches. Our boundaries need to be clear to avoid losing our autonomy.

While many people feel victimized by their past, there are also many people with similar experiences who do not react catastrophically and who seem to absorb the conflict and move forward unencumbered. Why is this the case? What accounts for individual differences?

A boy who witnesses the physical or emotional battering of his mother may either treat women in the same degrading fashion, decide never to show any signs of anger even when it might be justified, or learn to react and interact with a whole alternative gamut of responses. If a man chooses to deny his impulses without understanding why, he may become legitimately immobilized. Often this type of man defers to the woman, internalizes his anger, and expresses it in passive-aggressive behaviors. This safety valve, while temporarily quelling the emotion, eventually erodes the relationship. The corollary of a passive-aggressive male is an emotionally overwrought female. She cannot confront the man because his negative behavior is so well disguised. This disguised anger can become an habituated response, generalized to all relationships that threaten his comfort. Not dealing with anger erodes a person's self-image. Suppressing anger is not satisfying and leaves residual feelings of inadequacy.

Anger is not the only emotional response that can induce fear of expression. Many adolescents, struggling with raging hormones, have fantasies and desires that compel them to action. If a friend describes someone who is highly sexual, a fantasy begins. Given the opportunity to take advantage of the situation, the adolescent may experience anxiety, conflict over parental and religious admonitions, concern about poor sexual performance, and fear of pregnancy. These combine to stifle sexual expression. This was particularly true in past generations when sex before marriage was unacceptable and morally reprehensible.

The above examples depict a technique of highlighting a patient's negative experiences and tendencies that restrict the expression of emotion.

Insight offers pathways to healthy decision making in interpersonal relationships. Tony's difficulties resulted from a combination of his genetic predisposition, his temperament, and his emotional sensitivity due to mood fluctuations that began in early childhood. At a critical, negative stage in his life, he was without the internal resources, and formerly successful defensive maneuvers to combat his overwhelming stress. Neither Tony nor any of us is immune to the emotional turmoil that stress creates. Given the right circumstances, even the strongest among us may succumb to inordinate stressors. These circumstances and distorted internal perceptions are ripe for the development of victimization. Being a victim takes many forms. In Tony's therapy, I had to constantly remind him of his failure to assess past events properly, and to avoid seeing himself as a victim.

In chapter 7, I explained how stress alters brain chemistry. This can be ameliorated by psychotropic medication prescribed in combination with cognitive behavioral therapy. In the not-so-distant past, people suffering with debilitating symptoms of Obsessive Compulsive Disorder (OCD) were often consigned to mental institutions. The discovery of various psychotropic medications and improved therapeutic interventions has greatly lessened the need for hospitalization.

Imagine how good you would feel and think if you understood the origins of your negative actions and reactions. Good and bad motivations that we become aware of in psychotherapy allow us to access and to assess the real possibility of accomplishing more, thus maximizing our potential. This has an immensely positive effect on our self-esteem.

Tony

Psychotherapy taught me that life is a continuous growth and change process. I had denied both the positive and negative experiences from my childhood when I became a teacher, husband, and father. My journey of self-discovery in therapy made it possible for me to unlock my difficult memories. I hope I have provided a clear picture of the issues that led to my taking a leave of absence, and that Dr. Guido's analysis has made you aware that there are techniques and tools to overcome feeling alone, helpless and unhappy.

A PATH TO SELF-UNDERSTANDING

- Can you identify life experiences that unnecessarily and repeatedly lead to frustration?

- Do your reactions to these experiences contribute to your low self-esteem? What have you learned from the preceding chapters that may help you prevent these negative reactions in the future?

- Can you identify the internal resources that led to some of your successes?

- Did you experience guilt and shame when you were unsuccessful at trying to fit the mold imposed by your parents and others?

13

TAKING LIFE AND OURSELVES TOO SERIOUSLY
THE IMPORTANCE OF HUMOR
ITS CONTRIBUTION IN COGNITIVE RESTRUCTURING
AND BEHAVIORAL CHANGE

I can see what a laugh can do. It can transform almost unbearable tears into something bearable, even hopeful

-BOB HOPE

MANY PEOPLE TAKE themselves too seriously. The downside of this is the anxiety that occurs when trying to make over-the-top plans, choices, and decisions with a certainty that seldom exists. The more we agonize and over-analyze, the greater our confusion. It is unfortunate that this approach, which dominates our assessments, is the result of societal standards. Society imposes its truth on us. We may not agree with it. It is important to convey to patients that suggestions from others, as well as those that we make to others, are not commands.

Agreeing to disagree is a more productive way to communicate. In the end, it is healthier to make our own choices and not to rely solely on those of others. Creative parenting, good teaching, and high-quality psychotherapy need to be directed toward educating people to think for themselves. Psychological health is the result of coming to our own conclusions. Omnipotence and omniscience are qualities attributable to the gods, not to us mere mortals!

I often recount personal anecdotes that caused me awkwardness or embarrassment in order to highlight my own humanity. I relate decisions I made in my early adult life that required me to delay gratification. While I was a Teaching Fellow at St. John's University, I needed to supplement my income by working in a pizza parlor as a delivery boy, kitchen helper, etc. Many of my friends were buying houses and new cars. I knew that the quality of my life would improve when I completed my education.

I always try to convey that self-esteem includes the ability to laugh at ourselves. I encourage humor, which I introduce very early in therapy. I begin the process of building our therapeutic relationship with my own humorous experiences. This teaches patients to accept their humanity. They become comfortable with their reality. They feel free to reject the image they have spent years projecting to others. By hearing me retell my own similar experiences in a self-deprecating, humorous vein, my patients appreciate my willingness to expose my vulnerability, and to make fun of myself. When they listen to me relate a potentially embarrassing and painful situation, patients begin to feel free to reassess their own experiences and to find the positive value therein.

This cognitive restructuring of their memory provides them with an opportunity to see the value of reassessing negative past events from a different, more positive perspective. It allows them time to focus on positive recollections and experiences rather than immersing themselves in negative reminders and disappointments. Modeling the use of humor for your children when they perceive that an experience is negative, teaches them to laugh at themselves. Healthy laughter reduces anxiety and increases self-acceptance.

Not knowing I had an Attention Deficit Disorder, I felt inadequate in public Junior and Senior high school, less so when I was in Catholic elementary school because of the structure it provided. When I was in second grade, I feigned illness for more than two months because of a maniacal nun. Even as a child, I could intuitively identify a mentally dysfunctional person.

In my senior year of high school, I decided to go to college. Unfortunately, due to my ADD, my grades did not reflect my intelligence. I was accepted to college on probation. I proudly made the Dean's List during my first 19-credit semester by isolating myself in the dorm on the weekends, rewriting class notes, seeking help from the professors, and realizing that I was an auditory learner. I went on to earn a teaching assistantship for my 60 credit MA, and a teaching fellowship for my PhD.

Attention Deficit Disorder does not go away. I am still distractible in an unstructured setting. I am extremely focused with patients in my quiet office. I constantly lose or misplace my office and car keys. I sometimes forget to put an appointment in my phone calendar. I have embraced this deficit. I tell my patients that I easily lose track of time or forget to have a bill ready for them. They appreciate my honesty and they understand my issues. My patients with ADD learn to approach it differently. If their children have ADD, they understand the symptoms, learn how to be supportive in a constructive way, and demand advocacy in the school to insure proper remediation.

My wife, who has experienced my distractibility for many years and is of sound mind, still does not totally believe that I cannot always control it!

Recently she went to a pet store, purchased two dog ID tags, one for my office keys and one for my car keys. They are printed with the following message: "If found, please call: (123) 456-7890." I show them to my patients to lessen their embarrassment about similar behaviors.

When I asked if he had ever laughed at himself, Tony recalled a college fraternity hazing experience. He had completely blocked this event until my question prompted him to access the memory in therapy.

Tony

I thought of an incident that occurred at age 18 during my five-day fraternity hazing. Each of the pledges had to wear a costume. I was a hobo with a shoeshine box. At the end of hazing, I had to cut holes in my shoes to expose my red polished toenails, get on a subway at 42nd Street in full costume during rush hour, and sing the Downtown Strutters' Ball in English and Italian.

I was anxious about the public's reaction. I knew that a fraternity brother would be present if I needed help. The train doors closed. I got the signal to start. The subway train was packed. I began singing, "I'll be down to get you in a taxi, honey." Everyone looked at me and began to laugh. Their laughter undercut my anxiety. I continued. I began to sing the verses in Italian. I became aware of a hidden part of me. I believe that I became a raconteur in the classroom, with friends, and with family because of this.

Recounting the story in therapy provided Tony with an understanding of the admonition: "Don't take yourself too seriously!" Tony saw the value of looking for and finding positive outcomes in anticipated negative experiences.

Years later, when economic necessity forced Tony to seek a second job at an Italian restaurant, the initial unskilled tasks, dishwashing, extracting clams from their shells, and others did not feel demeaning. He was not concerned with his image. He felt a sense freedom and enjoyment in the restaurant. Tony began assisting the chef and creating the menus. He prepared many of the meals. This put him in touch with another dimension of his personality and an untapped skill. Cooking has been wonderful, creative and rewarding. Friends, family, neighbors, and a large fraternal organization all appreciate and anticipate the meals he prepares.

In therapy, Tony mentioned the name of the restaurant. It turned out that it had been one of our favorite restaurants. My wife and I, Italians who know good Italian food, loved the menu. I had no idea that Tony was the chef. A small world indeed!

A Path to Self-Understanding

- Name a situation in which you took yourself too seriously. What prompted you to be serious in the first place?

- As your situation played itself out, were the results humorous or not?

- What was the turning point that made it humorous?

- What did you learn about yourself?

- Can you imagine moments when a mindset might influence feelings of joy or anxiety? Can you use this insight to effect change in your overall disposition? Why?

- How could you use a humorous anecdote, interpretation, or insight to lessen the stress of others?

TONY'S ROAD TO HEALING AND TRANSFORMATION:
A MESSAGE OF PERSONAL RENEWAL

Twenty years ago, during the first phase of my therapy, I learned effective ways to overcome the inertia that drained meaning from my life. For me, psychotherapy has been enlightening, healing, and life changing. The validation of my strengths and my deepest desires has been rewarding. Learning about myself provides alternative responses when confronted by my own negativity.

My negative thought patterns that were both debilitating and empowering were identified. I learned the tools of cognitive behavioral restructuring to master new responses. In therapy, Dr. Guido and I developed strategies that helped me reframe the ways in which I interpreted my experiences. The tools and techniques of cognitive behavioral therapy have been crucial for me. They allow me to modify my ingrained, self-deprecating patterns. My challenge is to overcome my strong resistance to change through the judicious application of these strategies.

Therapy provides a safe-haven in which to express memories and concerns that are filled with guilt and shame. My professional relationship with Dr. Guido encouraged me to reveal personal experiences. It was gratifying that he was always aware of my need to find answers to my everyday struggles. He continually sees the beneficial effects of learning from his patients. Several of the diagrams in the book come from my extensive reading and have been integrated into the body of Between the Lines.

Dr. Guido set appropriate boundaries so that we could safely share our formative memories. He diffused my negative self-perceptions and helped me change them into positive self-acceptance. His ability to identify harmful, personal traits, rooted in my history, helped me become aware of my tendency to repeat my reactions.

Awareness is key. Psychotherapy offered me alternatives to enhance my interpersonal relationships. I believe that cognitive behavioral restructuring helped me confront the tensions of my life and move forward. As you read this part of Between the Lines, *I hope that you will be able to relate my struggle to your own life. If there is one message I wish to impart, it is that transformation is possible and you are not alone.*

PART 3

ADDITIONAL PSYCHOTHERAPEUTIC TECHNIQUES THAT ENHANCE THE BENEFITS OF COGNITIVE BEHAVIORAL THERAPY

14

Hypnosis/Desensitization Techniques To Overcome Habit Disturbances, Phobias and Addictions

When you know all parts of your personality, you can place your will between their impulses and your actions.

-Gary Zukav and Linda Francis

In parts 1 and 2 of *Between the Lines,* I explained the usefulness of cognitive behavioral therapy to enhance the quality of life. The underlying theme was to take the mystery out of psychotherapy and to free the reader of the negative view that psychotherapy is reserved for the mentally ill. True, some patients do have very debilitating mental illnesses, but the majority of people, though depressed, anxious, and/or severely stressed, can maximize their innate strengths and abilities by seeking help.

A competent and experienced therapist works with greater efficiency by learning various ancillary techniques that help patients with habit disturbances, addictions, and phobias to enjoy life without fear of re-crimination. Self-control, for example weight loss, needs to be a personal decision and not one tied to the dictates or comments of others. When we decide to modify our mental functioning based on outside pressures, we often sabotage ourselves. There are a number of possibilities that determine our addictive behaviors:

- An unclear boundary that creates the belief that our autonomy is being compromised. This compels us to continue self-defeating behaviors.

- The perceived belief that emotional emptiness can only be satisfied by self-indulgences that are often detrimental

- Genetic, learned, and socioeconomic behaviors

When people truly reach a decision to alter their lifestyle because their symptoms are interfering with their happiness and peace of mind, they are more likely to succeed. There is an innate striving for autonomy, which starts in early childhood and continues throughout life. Unclear boundaries trigger a need to please others because we are hoping to feel less rejected and alone.

HYPNOSIS/DESENSITIZATION:
ANCILLARY TO COGNITIVE BEHAVIORAL THERAPY

I became certified in hypnosis early in my career. I incorporate relaxation techniques of hypnosis and biofeedback for stress-related illnesses.

Hypnosis is often seen as a form of entertainment. Most people are not aware that hypnosis is a deep form of relaxation. A patient under hypnosis, while experiencing distortions of time and place, is conscious of the surroundings. If explained in this way, the fear of being controlled is usually alleviated. It is the therapist's job to create an atmosphere of trust before using hypnotic techniques. The entire process requires the therapist to listen carefully and to hear the patient's concerns. Depending on these concerns, more detail about the process may be necessary to reduce the patient's anxiety. The patient benefits more when an alliance exists with the therapist. At the same time, there are those patients who willingly enter into the hypnotic state to escape reality.

What is Desensitization?

All of us, at one time or another, have used this technique to combat our fears. When children are afraid of the dark, parents learn to keep a hallway light on for reassurance. As time passes, they place a night light in the room. The child's fear slowly dissipates. The feeling of mastery is internalized. This leads to the child sleeping in the dark.

Lazarus says:
Desensitization is most commonly indicated in overcoming persistent avoidance responses to innocuous events and situations. There is no objective reason for people to fear walking through a supermarket, riding in an elevator, eating in a restaurant, going to a beauty parlor, asking questions in class, seeing an ambulance, or hundreds of other petty fears and foibles which seriously incapacitate certain individuals.

He goes on to make the following observation:
Thus, even many classical phobias call for social and personal intervention in addition to, and sometimes in place of, systematic desensitization. Again, I find that these inconsistencies are better treated by methods of rehearsal, role playing and the use of rational-emotive therapy (Ellis, 1962). The net result following, say, role playing or the correction of faulty attitudes is

desensitization in that the patient no longer overreacts to innocuous events.

There are circumstances in therapy whereby switching roles allows a patient to hear a better form of communication. The therapist assumes the role of the patient while the patient role-plays the child, spouse, boss, co-worker, etc. By listening to a clearer, less harsh, or confrontational communication, and one that is more empathic, the patient learns a valuable lesson in communication. This provides the patient with different words to express his or her feelings and concerns. It is always helpful to find a caring way to talk to another person. I make certain the patient understands that what is important is the essence of the interpersonal exchange, listening *between the lines* of what is being said.

I use desensitization, as an ancillary technique to cognitive behavioral therapy, to help a patient confront specific fears and phobias. The goal of hypnosis in therapy is to create a state of deep relaxation while the patient remains aware and is able to communicate. Prior to the first desensitization session, in order to confront patients' fears, I ask them to identify the least anxiety-ridden thought connected to their fear, and its most dreaded aspect. For example, a patient who is afraid to fly, often experiences terror during lift-off or descent prior to landing. Each patient's areas of concern will vary depending on previous experiences. Some people have never flown, some have had terrifying experiences on a plane, and some may be reacting to negative descriptions from friends or the media.

The first image presented might be buying the tickets for a flight. As the patient imagines the task, I am able to monitor the degree of anxiety experienced, and provide reassurance using predetermined images. My patient has previously focused on being in a place that provides a sense of serenity. Using this image, I am able to redirect the fear until the anxiety dissipates entirely. The patient's guided imagery continues until mastery over the most anxiety-ridden image is overcome. Once this has occurred, a myriad of other suggestions are presented to reinforce the feeling of mastery.

I am intrigued when prospective patients ask me if they can be hypnotized to change behaviors that require intense therapy. Some want to be brought back in time to identify a past life. My use of hypnosis is reserved to augment desensitization to relieve anxiety, phobias, and habit disturbances. I am a therapist concerned with uncovering those experiences and feelings in an individual's history that provide clues to present behaviors and concomitant defense mechanisms determining behavior. For example, highly motivated patients, who would like to lose weight, can gain more control over their eating habits through hypnotic suggestion. But they still need to exert efforts to do so.

A patient was concerned about gaining weight after giving birth to her first child. There were a number of marital issues creating additional anxiety. Before using hypnosis to reinforce her commitment to lose weight and start a fitness program, I used a relaxation technique 1) to help this patient to control her anxiety and 2) as a precursor to hypnosis.

I mentioned previously that I never discount the possibility of a physical abnormality that may be the primary cause of a symptom. After a full physical including a gynecological examination, she was diagnosed with a cancerous tumor the size of a soccer ball. The cancerous tumor was removed, and chemotherapy was initiated. I continued to see the patient who was experiencing nausea and vomiting not only after treatment, but also on the way to the hospital in anticipation of chemotherapy. I used hypnosis and desensitization combined with cognitive restructuring to lessen these symptoms and to control both her anticipatory and reactive nausea and vomiting. I suggested that she would derive even more benefit if she listened to the recorded desensitization session that I had provided. My patient learned that listening to this recording was helpful not only at home, but also on her way to the hospital, and during her chemotherapy treatments. Because of the regular use of desensitization, in therapy and elsewhere, she was better able to tolerate the chemo-therapy treatments.

Hypnosis is often, but not always, a helpful technique for mastery of habit disturbances and addictions.

Many of us have difficulty controlling poor eating habits. This is one of the most common forms of addiction. Americans tend to separate poor eating habits from other more detrimental addictions like nicotine. The fact that eating is essential for survival allows us to deny the importance of controlling it. Morning news programs often include a segment on diet and exercise. The expert television personality feeds the frenetic eating-addicted consumer with solutions that are all painfully similar and ineffective. The media have made us believe that we need to spend inordinate amounts of time and money pursuing the perfect body. These self-anointed diet and exercise gurus convince us to remain vigi-lant about losing weight and staying fit. Diet and fitness have become multi-billion dollar industries.

Once we acknowledge this, we need to identify therapeutic strategies that motivate change.

- What other behaviors are influenced by brain interactions?

- To what extent are we able to change?

- Given our brain's resistance to alter behavior, what strategies can we use to overcome the inertia and create new behaviors?

ANECDOTE

Emma, a 40-year-old wife and mother, reached a point of difficulty sustaining a moderate exercise and food management program. During her 30s, she gradually lost her appealing physical attributes. By the time she turned 40, Emma was overweight and sluggish. Her former energetic, lively self was a thing of the past. No degree of reassurance from her husband, friends, and family helped her be less self-conscious. Her normally sharp thought processes diminished. A physical examination revealed hypertension with a borderline diabetic condition. She had ignored the warning signs.

Old photographs revealed that, in her 20s, Emma was shapely and vibrant. I asked her to bring in a photograph taken when she was physically at her best. This image was used with a series of other hypnotic suggestions to maintain her motivation. While we can never totally go back to the same physique, such images, coupled with the sense of good physical health, can bolster our desire to look and feel better.

- Why did reality hit now?

- Why had previous attempts to lose weight failed?

- How can hypnosis, desensitization, and cognitive restructuring help maintain a motivation after many years of failure?

Emma is only one of many of us who face similar issues. Our experiences are different but the net result is the same. Unfortunately, certain habits seem to gain control over our best interests and intentions? Whether caused by stress, boredom, depression, convenience, cultural or genetic factors, comfort level, or medication, the origins have to be identified. Only then can we determine a strategy to regain control.

Fortunately, some of us are successful.

- Do the differences between men and women determine the outcomes?

- Do we find excuses to sabotage the resolve to eat a proper diet and maintain an exercise program?

- Do we substitute fast foods because our schedules are too busy?

- Do we have business lunches that include alcohol and high calorie desserts?

- Do we watch too many over-the top food shows that encourage the delectability of high calorie meals and desserts?

There is tremendous pressure from the media to sustain an unrealistic lifestyle in order to feel young and stay healthy. In reality, we are constantly bombarded with negative stressors. I tell patients that the simplest road to maintaining control is to eat a healthy diet and determine an appropriate exercise routine. There are no quick fixes to the inevitable aging and metabolic changes that affect our minds and our bodies, despite the media hype.

There are also physiological components that must be considered and dismissed before undertaking therapeutic strategies for weight-loss. This follows my continued emphasis on ruling-out physiological causes for perceived psychological issues. An inner dialog, whether in therapy or on your own, is the key to liberating yourself from the destructive cycles in your life.

A Path to Self—Understanding

- Based on the content of this chapter, what insight have you gained about your life's journey?

- Identify a situation in your life that, at first, had negative implications that changed when you took the risk and did it anyway?

- Identify a behavior that disturbs you and requires change.

- What untapped inner resource or personality traits can kick start a positive change?

- What are the triggers that interfere with your behavior and cause you to maintain the negative behavior?

- What strategies are needed to hold the triggers in check?

- Can you be aware of the temptation to engage in other compulsive behaviors that mask a healthy solution?

- What may be needed to reinforce your original determination to overcome a negative habit?

- Are you be willing to seek a specific workshop or support group to overcome the negative behavior?

- Is your journey complete? Or do you need to continue to challenge yourself?

15

ANOTHER AVENUE TO LEARN ABOUT YOURSELF
SELF-DISCOVERY THROUGH DREAMS

I am more and more convinced that our happiness or unhappiness depends more on the way we meet the events of life than on the nature of those events themselves

-ALEXANDER HUMBOLDT

I AM FASCINATED BY the usefulness of interpreting patients' dreams as an adjunct to therapy. A dream that I had early in my own second course of therapy became an important theme for me.

MY DREAM

I awoke from the dream with a strong feeling of depression, marked sadness, and an immobilizing heaviness as if I were shouldering the burdens of the world. I was a small child in an apartment that belonged to a friend's family. I was extremely upset and was headed toward my parents' bedroom seeking reassurance. My mom was seated in bed in an evening gown. A pillow supported her. Her hair was brushed, she wore red lipstick, and a folded blanket covered the lower part of her body. She indicated that I should come forward. Upon reaching her, I rested my head on her, expecting a hug. All she could do to pat my head in a manner devoid of any real nurturing. My father continued to sleep.

Still dreaming, I was suddenly on a sidewalk looking at my aunt's house. It was an exact image of a tenement building where my sister, my brother, and I lived while our mother was gravely ill after surgery. As the dream continued, I was desperate to cross the street. I was frightened to run because of the oncoming traffic. My fear was intense. I felt immobilized, as if I would never get to my aunt's house.

The content was symbolic of the origins of the emotional disconnectedness I felt from my mother whose surgical procedure was so complicated and traumatic that she went into a psychotic episode. My friend's apartment in my dream represented my home. In real time, my siblings and I never knew anything about our mother's illness. The separation anxiety and deep depression that I felt are as real today as they were then. My aunt, uncle, and three older cousins embraced and nurtured us. This was the very first time that I experienced unconditional love. I knew I had found an extremely safe haven despite the cramped quarters of that apartment.

My need for nurturance and my fear of loss interfered with forming healthy interpersonal relationships. I was plagued with separation anxiety. I needed to address my lack of boundaries and my need to merge. This understanding prompted me to learn more about dream interpretation so that I could be more effective with my patients.

Using Dreams In Therapy

Tony was amazed with the revelation that dreams enhance insight and help process conflict. Dreams taught Tony how his life experiences influenced the way he thought and felt and why paying attention to our dreams often leads to insight. Tony gained more depth and understanding through the interpretation of the following dream.

Tony

I was traveling on a road at my leisure. A pedestrian flagged me down and told me that I had to get home because someone was in danger. I was driving up a mountainous road, pushing myself to get home, and feeling tremendous stress. Suddenly the highway came to an abrupt end. I was launched into space, free falling over an ocean, fighting to get out of the car. The car plunged further into the water. I escaped by kicking out the window. I woke up. I was relieved that it was only a dream.

I used this opportunity to point out that the objects and individuals in a dream represent different parts of us. In Tony's dream, the person in the car was enjoying the decision to take pleasure in solitude, a rare experience for Tony. The car represented the parts of Tony's personality that kept trying to move forward, only to be thwarted. In certain circumstances, Tony experienced conflict around the need to seek social intimacy and attachment. His detachment led to his persistent feeling of obligation, which also defined his self-esteem. Tony's inability to interact successfully resulted in his feelings of inadequacy.

Vehicles served as metaphors for Tony's navigation through life. The vehicles, cars, bicycles, roller coasters, and buses, became dangerous rather than reliable forms of entertainment, leisure, and practicality.

Tony understood that, prior to the free-fall he was experiencing in the dream, his energy was depleted. This feeling of uncertainty was consistent throughout Tony's life. The need to pursue an ideal caused internal conflict. In his dream, Tony heard that his family was in danger. He could not anticipate what lay ahead. He wanted to avoid pain. Tony's personal conflicts drained his energy whenever he tried to accomplish the ideal.

Tony was phobic about water. He had not learned to swim. He felt unable to survive in deep water. He avoided swimming pools. Plunging into water aroused his fear of death and underscored his failure to rescue a family member. Tony's need to rise to the occasion yet remain in his comfort zone often immobilized him. When he kicked out the car window, he freed himself. He learned that he could be resourceful in the face of fear and conflict. He finally integrated what was pointed out in our very first session: therapy is a path to identify our strengths and to reconcile our weaknesses.

In spite of his shortcomings and negative mindset, Tony mastered many challenges throughout his life. I explained to Tony that dreams often reflect our present day conflicts. In the final analysis, we have the resources to overcome the preconceived concern about our demise. The dream process is the brain's attempt to resolve conflict, to keep us in balance.

Tony

I realized that the dream occurred after my wife requested that I find a doctor in Florida. I had been avoiding a consultation and physical examination. My retirement, the pleasant journey in my car, was interrupted. The stranger was warning that I might be in danger if I avoided health issues. Though my motivation to succeed had helped me accomplish numerous goals, I did not draw upon my strength. I continued to anticipate failure and disappointment. The insecurity of not knowing what lay ahead was always present when I was stressed. I had decided to discontinue my medication a number of years before the dream. This increased my vulnerability.

The common thread for all of us is the stifling need to defend against negative outcomes. This defense has the power to overwhelm and thwart spontaneity. Obsessive worry, common to everyone in one degree or another, requires new behavioral and emotional responses. These are difficult to master when we have developed the self-protective need for hypervigilance, excessive analysis, and the defensiveness that creates the pinball effect. (V: Chapter 7) These ego-driven characteristics, used in excess, do not solve the basic problem. They actually fuel the fire. A person's ego is ferocious, always wanting more affirmation of self-importance and strength. The therapist helps the patient discover and develop new pathways. You cannot solve a problem using the same mindset that caused it.

Tony

Dr. Guido suggested that my strong resources helped me survive in the face of opposition. We focused on my passions. I enjoyed the exhilaration of pitching a 1-0 shutout in a playoff game, of teaching my students mathematics and witnessing their growth, of having a part-time job and learning to cook, of teaching religious education, and of being husband and father to my wife and six children. I learned that everyone has underlying energy and talents that may not be obvious. This helped in my parenting and my teaching. I learned to draw out, recognize, and reinforce the potential strength in others.

I emphasized in Tony's therapy that there are underlying causes for many forms of resistance. Psychotherapy helped Tony discover that those were the polarization of his true self vs. his false sense of self. He learned to identify the outside forces that prevented the integration of these disparate aspects of his personality. Tony always felt that he had to modify his thinking and behavior to conform to the expectations of society. The pedestrian in the dream represented outside influences that trigger the questioning and self-monitoring Tony used defensively. Should he selfishly pursue what he wanted and feel guilty, or learn from his choices? Tony discovered that changes in his behavior were possible by extracting knowledge from these events. He finally acknowledged that we each have the right to make choices, as long as we take full responsibility for them. Our need for autonomy must, at times, override the fear of recrimination.

People frequently feel guilt and shame stemming from a black or white mentality. Tony realized that he had to integrate the disparate parts of his personality: the moral, upstanding husband, father, and teacher with the unfortunate, misguided, compliant person riddled with doubt and anxiety. Without reconciliation, Tony would spend the remainder or his life judging himself harshly. Tony needed space to maintain his balance in life. He felt disapproval from his wife and several of his children. Perhaps his needs to be dependable, and to rise to the occasion, enabled their dependency on him, and, at the same time, created their disapproval and resentment.

Tony learned that the problem for all of us is our tendency to be plagued by conscious decisions that are often guided by unconscious wishes. Cognitive behavioral therapy offers us routes to connect unconscious motivations with present day decision-making. These insights can become a permanent restructuring of our thinking if we continue to work on our awareness of the need to understand and to modify the basis of our decision-making. This is a truly freeing experience, a complete acceptance of who we are and how we are perceived.

Insights Gained from Tony's Dream Interpretations

- In addition to the car's trunk containing the personal baggage of repeated negative mindsets, the faceless stranger evokes the fundamental conflict between satisfying personal needs or feeling an obligation to others.

- Uncertainty ensues and fuels the fire of anxiety and obsessive rumination, leading to the triggering of the amygdala hijack. (V: Chapter 7) This intensifies anxiety arousal and a distortion of reality.

- The sudden loss of serenity, of satisfying a much-needed pleasurable experience, leads to a perceived loss of control.

- A separation between purpose and loss of control compounds the mistaken belief that satisfying one's own needs often leads to negative outcomes or an inability to separate anxiety from reality.

- Insight in therapy breaks through, symbolically, by kicking out the glass window, and frees our internal resources of self-preservation. We do not always have to be self-sacrificing. If we develop a sense of inner-balance, the disparity in need systems becomes clearer and less intense.

A Path to Self—Understanding

- What influence has life had in your dreams?

- Are you willing to acquire knowledge about your personality through dream analysis?

- Using our definition of the symbolic nature of dreams, are you able to determine the personal significance of images represented in your dreams? (e.g. The car in Tony's dream was a symbol of confinement, a negative mindset that prevented his release.)

- What symbolism in your dreams has created a disparity between what you desire, and what you perceive as necessary?

- Elusive or not, can you identify redeeming qualities in your personality that are the source of your greatest strengths? Once identified, how can they help you reframe the way you think, and deal with stress, anger, anxiety, depression, and other emotional states?

16

I Believe ... that our background and circumstances may have influenced who we are, but we are responsible for whom we become.

-Anonymous

A s I wrote *Between the Lines*, I tried to emphasize the importance of being in charge of your own life. I used phrases like "embrace your weaknesses as well as your strengths", "be less reactive to life's stressors", "take charge of difficult negative experiences," "convert negative thoughts into positive ones to lessen your anxiety" and the "only person you can control is yourself."

I specifically wanted to take the mystery out of psychotherapy. I used my self-revelations to enhance the reader's understanding of what led me to develop my own brand of therapy. To that end, I hope to empower beginning therapists and non-therapists to break down certain barriers that are often the result of people denying their own belief system.

Patients feel more comfortable knowing that therapists have had similar life experiences. Knowledge gained through coursework and supervised training is not enough. I use cognitive behavioral therapy successfully in my practice. I believe that, by embodying some facets of other treatment styles, cognitive behavioral therapy is the most effective and eclectic form of therapy. I integrate some aspects of these other modalities that are integral to my personal style. Other successful methods of psychotherapy have helped numerous people. What works for me may not be the perfect therapeutic model for all therapists. The choice must be a function of the individual therapist's knowledge and comfort level.

I wanted to convey the importance of boundary setting in my work and in my personal life. It took me a long time to recognize that poor boundaries confound all of our interpersonal relationships, both in the therapy setting and in life. Blurred boundaries affect our ability to remain objective. We encounter serious relationship problems when we cannot distinguish our needs from the expectations of family, friends, co-workers, and other important persons. No one is immune to the conflicted and confusing emotions that stem from interpersonal relationships. I learned how to create consistent boundaries by observing and analyzing my patients' lives and my own. Boundaries enhance the quality of life for each of us, regardless of age.

Many of us choose to go into treatment as a result of unclear interpersonal boundaries that interfere with our ability to control our feelings, make us feel victimized, and allow us to project our insecurities onto others. When we give up control and lose sight of our boundaries, we are no longer in control of our own lives. We must each learn more about our need to own our faulty reasoning, our confused feelings, and our behaviors, in order to resolve our stress. This is imperative for our peace of mind.

In my teaching and my life, I have come to understand the importance of the physiology of stress. I was taught to believe the metaphoric definition of "mind" and "psyche", and that my "mind" dictated the course of my life. In truth, the brain, an organ of our bodies, is the storehouse of pathways that control every aspect of our thinking and functioning, both psychological and physiological. I, too, had to learn how to control stress, despite all of my knowledge and training as a psychologist. Thirty years ago, I was diagnosed with a duodenal inflammation that sent me to the emergency room three times because the effects of indigestion mimicked a heart attack. This situation forced me to re-evaluate my lifestyle. I joined a fitness center and running club to help me learn to relax and let go. My symptoms never recurred.

My growing knowledge of the physiology of stress took the mystery out of its dynamics, its influence on brain chemistry, and its dire consequences. I taught a university course on the subject. This has had a profound influence on my work with patients. Preparing the course brought me up-to-date with the latest research into the physiology of stress, and the positive effects of psychotropic medications. When I recommend that a patient needs to consult a psychopharmacologist, I devote as much time as needed to assuage the patient's anxiety. I provide detailed explanations, with diagrams, showing how selective serotonin reuptake inhibitors (SSRIs) and medications that increase dopamine prevent the amassing of the brain chemicals that interfere with neurotransmission and help to redirect them in the brain.

In my long career as a psychotherapist, I have seen many changes in the ways we view and understand human psychology. As we continue to refine our understandings, we must adapt our beliefs to incorporate new paths for success. I have worked my way through the various therapies, from psychoanalysis to the present. It is clear to me that cognitive behavioral therapy offers the best chances for success in restructuring our lives. I know that, without my understanding of cognitive behavioral therapy, my professional and personal relationships would stagnate.

Tony, the patient whose case study I present in Part 2, chose therapy when he was convinced that no one and nothing could ever help him reclaim his serenity and confidence. Upon meeting him, I was able to provide him with hope. Tony was resistant to change, yet he proved a willing learner once he understood that his choices were not irrevocable and he had a great deal in common with others. I taught him to diffuse the power of his shame by talking about it. When he returned to therapy after 15 years, my first question after he expressed his mental anguish was, "When did you decide to discontinue your medication?" When he agreed to renew his medications, I was able to help him regain his sense of self.

Shedding light on our fears, makes them less potent. I have always known this intuitively. I learned about the research that supports it while studying clinical psychology. I have had the good fortune to help my many patients using my knowledge, my intuition, and my tenacity to identify the right course of treatment.

Many patients return to therapy during crises that develop in different phases of life. The previous alliance brings them back to see me, their trusted ally and therapist. The return to therapy is often short-term.

During my childhood, listening to the members of my dysfunctional family, I learned that humor was an effective way to take the sting out of emotional pain. While training to be a therapist, I found myself questioning whether their use of humor was constructive. I concluded that humor, used judiciously to ease some of the immediate emotional pain, could be very potent, if the underlying causes of the pain are dealt with openly and honestly. In *Between the Lines*, I have presented frightening, shameful, and anxiety-producing situations. During therapeutic interactions with all of my patients, I am continually aware of the importance of humor and its contribution to cognitive restructuring and behavioral change. I hope that I have succeeded in helping you understand that taking life and ourselves too seriously is detrimental to our quest for peace of mind.

The success of therapy is greater, if there are a number of ancillary techniques used to promote a healthy balance among the three major components of functioning: our mental state, our physiology, and our health. Cognitive behavioral therapy is always a necessary component in all aspects of treatment. Ancillary techniques like hypnosis, desensitization, and stress-management protocols depend on the successful use of cognitive behavioral therapy. All of our negative thoughts are intertwined with every aspect of our functioning. Remember: If you change the way you think, you change the way you feel, and, ultimately, you change the way you behave!

We can't change the wind ... but we can adjust our sails
-Anonymous

BETWEEN THE LINES
JOURNEYS OF SELF–REFLECTION:
APPROPRIATE INTERPERSONAL BOUNDARIES
AND ATTAINMENT OF PEACE OF MIND

I designed this summary to be read before reading *Between the Lines*. It will help you familiarize yourself with the content, and focus your attention on the salient points of the book. When I taught reading and study skills to high school seniors, I instructed them to start with the summary, which provides a framework for understanding the scope of the material.

PREFACE

Emotional issues can be modified in psychotherapy. A successful dialogue between patients and therapists provides the tools to attain peace of mind by redirecting thought processes. This leads to clarity of thought and takes the mystery and stigma out of psychotherapy.

INTRODUCTION

Between the Lines is a metaphor for the process of cognitive behavioral therapy. Average people may suffer psychological turmoil needlessly. Some real fears in our society may generate irrational thoughts that exert negative influences on our behaviors. Chapters 2 - 6 concentrate on boundary issues that affect our interpersonal relationships and lead to conflict. *Between the Lines* provides an understanding of the need for specific boundaries in our interpersonal relationships.

PART 1
BECOMING A PSYCHOLOGIST:
PRECURSORS IN MY JOURNEY THE IMPORTANCE OF BOUNDARIES
A DISCUSSION OF HEALTHY VS. UNHEALTHY PSYCHOLOGICAL DEVELOPMENT

CHAPTER 1
BECOMING A PSYCHOLOGIST
PRECURSORS TO MY JOURNEY

My choice to enter the field of psychology was influenced by the mental illness with which my family and I were confronted. My experiences as caregiver to mentally ill family members helped me develop my style of psychotherapy.

ADDITIONAL INSTANCES FROM MY OWN JOURNEY

I discuss my brain tumor, my psychological diagnoses, my therapy, and the ways I incorporated what I learned from each into my practice.

DEVELOPMENT OF MY SPECIFIC THERAPEUTIC STYLE

It is important to convey to patients that their emotional turmoil is not fixed and unchangeable. Successful psychotherapy enhances peace of mind. A therapist needs to be challenging in interactions with patients, while being aware of the impact of the dialogue. This requires setting firm boundaries. The choice of a therapist can make a difference between success and failure in psychotherapy. Understanding the physiology of stress and its impact on the body can motivate a person to alter behaviors. My belief is that all people are capable of improving their quality of life. Reality-oriented psychotherapy and suggested readings increase a patient's self-understanding. This, in turn, motivates change.

CHAPTER 2
PARENTING ISSUES:
A PROLOGUE OLDER CHILDREN STILL LIVING HOME

This chapter is the first of 5 that explore the origins of separation anxiety, the fears linked to our interpersonal relationships, and boundary issues that impede the independence of children. Neither the parents nor their adult children living at home know how to move forward. All of them are afraid to separate and grow.

THE HEAD IN THE SAND MENTALITY

When our anxiety overwhelms and controls our thinking, we cannot move forward. We become bogged down in a morass. Our every movement forces us deeper into the mire. Our feet are facing the sun and clarity, while our head and shoulders are buried deep in the sand. Without resolution, we will repeat our self-destructive patterns *ad infinitum*. True growth demands an understanding that we can control only our own behaviors and reactions.

CHAPTER 3
MILLENNIALS
UNDERSTANDING THE NEED FOR DEVELOPING NEW RULES OF PARENTING

As an outgrowth of the vast changes in our society during the1960s and 70s, dependence on parents stretched well beyond adolescence. Parents became aware of the dangers facing their children. Instead of teaching independence, the parents tried to give their children everything. Adults overreacted to teenagers who were being encouraged to think for themselves.

FIVE KEYS TO THE CREATIVE PROCESS

- Consumption

- Brainstorming

- Critical Thinking

- Incubation

- Production

The chart on page 10 clearly delineates how adults use their own needs to stifle their children's natural development.

A DIRECT APPLICATION OF COMMUNICATION SKILLS
FOSTERING GOOD PARENTING WORKSHOP NOTES:
BRIEF PRESENTATION TO PARENTS

Consistent with my beliefs that people need to be educated about parenting issues, I have provided the structure for a lecture that I use when I present a workshop on effective parenting.

CHAPTER 4
THE ORIGINS OF SIGNIFICANT CHANGES:
PARENTING STYLES IN THE NEW MILLENNIUM
CROSSING OVER FROM THE 1950s TO THE MILLENNIUM

More and more children in their late 20s and beyond are returning to live in their parents' home, impeding the heretofore natural progression of parents and their grown children through separation and into adulthood. Societal roles were changing. Self-indulgence was the mantra. Parenting and the family underwent many profound changes. We need to adjust our thinking in order to find ways for our children to become productive and leave home.

CHAPTER 5
WE THOUGHT IT WAS OUR HOUSE
TYPICAL SCENARIOS EXPERIENCED BY MANY PARENTS TODAY

In this chapter, I present 3 separate anecdotes that are concerned with issues confronting today's parents and their grown children. I provide some insights into the difficulties of parenting adult children who return to live at home. Every member of the family is looking for positive regard from every other family member. Parents and their adult children must work together to acknowledge their own issues and to develop successful positive regard and respect.

VENN DIAGRAM
ILLUSTRATION OF UNSUCCESSFUL BOUNDARY SETTING

Figure 1 is a Venn diagram that represents the pitfalls encountered when parents and children have not arrived at mutually acceptable boundaries that delineate their interpersonal relationships. In the jargon of the 21st century, we call the hovering, older generation, "helicopter parents".

CHAPTER 6
WHY IT HAPPENED
POOR BOUNDARY SETTING

If we wish to succeed in life, we must set reasonable boundaries in all of our relationships. Guilt that stems from our children's reactions to our demands is destructive. If we make them too comfortable, our children will never leave home. Unclear boundaries cause confusion. Living at home, as an adult, requires participation in every aspect of upkeep. Adult children are not children. They must take responsibility for themselves. The second Venn diagram illustrates healthy interactions between adult children and their parents.

Recap

Parents and children must reevaluate their living arrangements. All members of the family need to be open to the growth and change that foster positive regard and respect.

Venn Diagram
Illustration of Successful Boundary Setting

Figure 2 illustrates how children and parents reach separation and individuation through cooperative, successful boundary setting. This is a process that starts at birth and matures as our children grow.

Chapter 7
An Understanding of the Physiology of the Brain
Effects of Prolonged Stress on Personality Functioning

This chapter briefly summarizes the deleterious effects of our physiology on our psychological health. Prolonged stress causes our systems to falter and autoimmune diseases may occur. Stress is the number one killer in our society. Acute stress disorders, like PTSD, are real but must be dealt with in order to lessen their impact on us. We are born with the abilities to adapt to environmental stimuli. If brain maturation is interrupted by chemical imbalances or negative parenting, conflict begins to occur and it becomes circular.

The Pinball Effect of the Amygdala Hijack

Figures 3 and 4 illustrate the pinball effect of the amygdala hijack. The amygdala is the part of our brain that remembers reactions to stimuli and feelings.

More about Obsessive Rumination

A brief look at initial brain development and a return to the need to set boundaries to prevent perseveration throughout life.

Part 2

Tony's Story

Learning cognitive restructuring in Successful Psychotherapy

Chapter 8

The First Phase of Therapy

Most of us, like Tony, seek psychotherapy only when we have reached a definitive impasse in life. Tony's story clearly shows how our minds hijack our successes without us understanding the process. Tony and I provide the background that led him to therapy. I discuss the tools of cognitive behavioral therapy and how to use them in therapy and at home. I define the real meaning of what occurs *Between the Lines* of our core beliefs and I help you understand that you alone are responsible for your decisions and that it is okay to change your mind.

Chapter 9

Victimization

How Ordinary Life Events Can Shape Behavior

We have all felt like victims at one time or another. Some of us feel victimized and marginalized most of the time. Tony fought an internal war between obsessive rumination and reality-oriented thinking. We must embrace our **emotional and cognitive dysfunction.** The emotional intensity that we transfer from an initial event will dictate our later life reactions if we do not harness them.

Reconciling Both Sides of the Coin

Tony had never resolved the childhood conflict of self-determination vs. defiance of authority. He was unable to individuate. I provide some provocative thoughts in the body of this chapter for your consideration. I explain the what-if mentality that paralyzes action. If we are not kind to ourselves, if we cannot satisfy our needs, we are incapable of providing nurturance and love to our families.

Chapter 10
More On Cognitive Restructuring
The Contribution of Self—Defeating Behaviors & Failure
Two Sides of the Coin Revisited

Cognitive behavioral therapy provides us with the tools needed for cognitive restructuring. It allows patients to reframe the emotional patterns that cause pain and suffering. In the first part of this chapter, I explain how Tony was able to use cognitive behavioral therapy to turn negative reactions into positive ones. I introduce the common concept I-want-what-I-want-when-I-want-it that handicaps our growth.

The Other Side of the Coin:
Further Insights in Accessing Inner Strength

Therapeutic insights help us identify repetitive, destructive patterns that re-emerge regularly in life. We need to use the tools of cognitive behavioral therapy to find our inner-strength.

Reading Between the Lines
Two Sides of the Coin and the Management of Stress

I have included a table that explains how you can overcome destructive thoughts and actions using the tools of cognitive behavioral therapy.

CHAPTER 11
DISTORTIONS, FALSE BELIEF PATTERNS, OBSESSIVE /
COMPULSIVE RITUALS TO PROTECT THE SELF

An explanation of cognitive restructuring using cognitive behavioral therapy techniques

TONY'S CLEAR AND INGRAINED MEMORIES

I take a brief look at some additional issues that caused Tony to feel like a victim and I explain how to use cognitive restructuring to move out of the victim mindset.

TONY'S FEAR OF TAKING MEDICATION:
AN OBSTACLE TO OVERCOME

I engage in an in-depth discussion of cognitive restructuring and its use to overcome life-long fears and phobias. The patient's distorted beliefs about psychotropic medications are clarified for resistive patients. The benefits outweigh the possible negative side effects reported in the media.

CHAPTER 12
MORE INSIGHTS AND THE CONTINUATION OF THE
DYNAMICS OF CHANGE
SELF–ACTUALIZATION IN PLACE OF STAGNATION
TRANSFORMATION FROM PAIN TO HEALING

I present several additional anecdotes that are explained by Abraham Maslow's *Hierarchy of Needs*. The successful use of tools of cognitive behavioral therapy allows adults to restructure their harmful, learned responses.

CHAPTER 13
TAKING LIFE AND OURSELVES TOO SERIOUSLY
THE IMPORTANCE OF HUMOR
ITS CONTRIBUTION IN COGNITIVE RESTRUCTURING AND BEHAVIORAL CHANGE

Society indicates how we should function. When we forget that we are human, we become anxious and depressed. Acceptance of who we are is the most important lesson in life. We need to learn to be kind to ourselves and to laugh at ourselves. Laughter mitigates many negative consequences. Tony recounts a fraternity-hazing prank that taught him to relax and enjoy the laughter. I end with a discussion of Tony's willingness to work at a restaurant when he needed more money.

TONY'S ROAD TO HEALING AND TRANSFORMATION:
A MESSAGE OF PERSONAL RENEWAL

Tony explains how I, Dr. Stephen Guido, and the tools of cognitive behavioral therapy, have helped him regain and maintain a positive perspective on life.

PART 3
ADDITIONAL PSYCHOTHERAPEUTIC TECHNIQUES THAT ENHANCE
THE BENEFITS OF COGNITIVE BEHAVIORAL THERAPY

CHAPTER 14
ADDITIONAL THERAPEUTIC STRATEGIES
HYPNOSIS/DESENSITIZATION:
ANCILLARY TO COGNITIVE BEHAVIORAL THERAPY

I became certified in hypnosis early in my career.

WHAT IS DESENSITIZATION?

I use desensitization to amplify the effects of cognitive behavioral therapy. In this chapter, I use examples to explain how these ancillary techniques help us learn to use the cognitive restructuring tools more effectively.

Chapter 15
Another Avenue to Learn About Yourself
Self–Discovery Through Dreams

Dream interpretation provides great insights into our personalities and our functioning. Dreaming is the mind's way of reconciling all conflict. I make reference to resistance and unconscious wishes in my dream interpretations and I emphasize that cognitive behavioral therapy offers us routes to connect unconscious motivations from our past to present day decision-making.

Insights Gained From Tony's Dream Interpretations

To help clarify dream interpretation, I repeat, in a list, the important insights gleaned from our discussions of Tony's dream.

Chapter 16
The Author's Reflections

In *Between the Lines,* I emphasize the importance of being in charge of your own life. I demystify psychotherapy. I explain how patients feel more comfortable knowing that therapists have had similar life experiences. I convey the importance of boundary-setting and how it impacts our peace of mind. I have adapted my practice to the many advances in the ways we view and understand human psychology and various therapeutic modalities. Throughout my long career, I have used my knowledge, my intuition and my tenacity to help many patients. I address frightening, shameful, and anxiety-producing situations. *Between the Lines* focusses on helping you understand that taking life too seriously is detrimental to your quest for peace of mind.

WORKS CITED

American Psychiatric Association. (2013). *Diagnostic and statistical manual of mental disorders: DSM-5™ (5th ed.).* Arlington, VA: American Psychiatric Publishing, Inc.

Beck, Aaron T., M.D. (1976) *Cognitive Therapy and Emotional Disorder,* Madison, CT: International Universities Press.

Department of Health (2001) Evidence-Based Clinical Practice. *Treatment Choice in Psychological Therapies and Counselling,* Crown Copyright

Eagle, Morris N. *From Classical to Contemporary Psychoanalysis: A Critique and Integration* (Book Review): Philadelphia, PA: Routledge Press

Ellis, Albert (1962) *Reason and emotion in psychotherapy,* Fort Lee, NJ: Lyle Stuart Publishing

Erikson, Erik H. (1993) *Childhood and Society,* New York, NY: W. W. Norton & Company

Girdano, Daniel, Dusek, Dorothy E., Everly, George S., Jr (1993). *Controlling Stress and Tension,* Englewood Cliffs, NJ: Prentice Hall

Goleman, Daniel (2012). *Emotional intelligence.* New York, NY: Bantam. Random House LLC

Handel, Steven (2013). The 5 key stages of the creative process. *The Emotion Machine*

Horwitz, Allan V. (2002). Outcomes for the Sociology of Mental Health and Illness: Where Have We Been and Where Are We Going? *Journal of Health and Social Behavior*, Vol. 43, No. 2, pp. 143-151 Hughes, Melody (n.d.), Retrieved from http://www.ehow.com

Lazarus, Arnold A. (1996). *Behavior therapy and beyond*, New York, NY: Jason Aronson, Inc.

Mantel, Michael, Albrecht, Steve. (1994) *Ticking Bombs: Defusing Violence in the Workplace*, Irwin Professional Pub: Burr Ridge, IL

Maslow, Abraham, H., (2011) *Toward a psychology of being*. Eastford, CT: Martino Fine Books

Masson, Jeffrey Moussaiff. (1990) *Final Analysis: The Making and Unmaking of a Psychoanalyst*, New York, NY: Addison-Wesley Publishing Company, Inc.

Robin, Arthur L., Foster, Sharon L (2002). *Negotiating Parent-Adolescent Conflict: A Behavioral-Family Systems Approach*, New York, NY: The Guilford Press

Simple Nursing (2013), Retrieved from http://SimpleNursing.com, p.6

U.S. Census Bureau. (2013) *Social and demographic trends*, Retrieved from http://www.pewsocialtrends.org

Bibliography

Albom, M. *(2002) Tuesdays with Morrie. New York, NY; Broadway Books. Random House LLC*

Bacal, H. (1998). *Optimal responsiveness: How therapists heal their patients.* Northvale, NJ: Jason Aronson Inc.

Brammer. L. M., & Shostrom, E. L. *Therapeutic Psychology: Fundamentals of Counseling and psychotherapy.* (1989). Englewood Cliffs, New Jersey: Prentice Hall, Inc.

Bourne, E. (2010). *The anxiety & phobia workbook.* Oakland, CA: New Harbinger Publications, Inc.

Cloud, H., & Townsend, J. (1992). *Boundaries: When to say yes, how to say no.* Grand Rapids, MI: Zondervan, HarperCollins Publishing

Didion, Joan, (2005). The year of magical thinking. New York: Vintage Press

Faber, A. & Mazlish, E. (2012). *How to talk so kids will listen & listen so kids will talk.* New York, NY: Scribner

Feldman, D. (1991). *Do penguins have knees?* New York, NY: HarperCollins Publishers, Inc.

Forsyth, J., & Eifert, G. (2008). *The mindfulness and acceptance workbook for anxiety.* Oakland, CA: New Harbinger Publications, Inc.

Freud, S. (2010). *The interpretation of dreams.* New York, NY: Basic Books, Inc.

Gaylin, W. (1984). *The rage within: Anger in modern life.* New York, NY: Simon & Schuster, Inc.

Hallowell, E., & Ratey, J. (2011). *Driven to distraction: Recognizing and coping with attention deficit disorder from childhood through adulthood.* New York, NY: Anchor Books.

Johnson, Robert A. (1986). *Inner work – using dreams and active imagination for personal growth.* New York, NY: Harper One

Jung, C. (1968). *Man and his symbols.* New York, NY: Dell, Random House

Jung, C. (2010). *Synchronicity: An acausal connecting principle.* Princeton, NJ: Princeton University Press.

Robin, A. & Foster, S. (2001). *Negotiating parent-adolescent conflict: A behavioral-family systems approach.* New York, NY: Grand Central Publishing

Sarno, J. (1998). *The mind body prescription: Healing the body, healing the pain.* New York, NY: Warner Books, Inc.

Schiff, H. (2012). *The bereaved parent.* New York, NY: Crown Publishers. Random House LLC

Seligman, M. (2006). *Learned optimism: How to change your mind and your life.* New York, NY: Vintage Books.

Wallerstein, J. & Blakeslee, S. (1996). *The good marriage: How & why love lasts.* New York, NY: Grand Central Publishing.

APPENDIX I.A.

MODELS OF INDIVIDUAL HEALTH BEHAVIOR

I included the following educational models to increase an understanding of elements of communication that enhance a variety of interpersonal relationships. The concepts listed are part of a curriculum for nurses. They can be applied to effective communication between people in any context. Boundary issues, personal biases, judgmental attitudes, and stress that lessens motivation to maintain empathy are simplified and augment the tenets of *Between the Lines.*

EMPATHY, COMMUNICATION, AND COUNSELING SKILLS:

MODELS OF INDIVIDUAL HEALTH BEHAVIOR

Human behavior includes affect, behavior, and cognitions

Models:

- health belief model: patients have certain beliefs based on what they value and expect

- your belief in a personal threat together with your belief in the effectiveness of the proposed treatment/behavior/lifestyle affects whether or not you seek that treatment/behavior/lifestyle

- explains rationale for not seeking medical care: don't believe they have an illness, don't see a benefit

- theory of planned behavior: attitude toward behavior, subjective norms, and perceived behavioral control, together shape an individual's behavioral intentions and behaviors

- trans theoretical model and stages of change: assesses an individual's readiness to act on a new healthier behavior, and provides strategies or processes of change to guide the individual through the stages of change to action and maintenance

- specific interventions are based on which stage the individual is in.

EMPATHY, COMMUNICATION, AND COUNSELING SKILLS: BACKGROUND

Terms:

- empathy: an intellectual identification with the feelings, thoughts, or attitudes of another where boundaries of the self are maintained

- results in increased understanding of the patient perspective without adopting their feelings

- skills in this may be a clinician's most important tool as it enhances effectiveness of care, improves patient satisfaction, and lessens disposition towards malpractice suits

- sympathy: a temporary loss of self-awareness in which one feels emotionally the feelings of another such that the boundaries of the self are not maintained

- results in increased understanding of patient perspective along with adoption of the same

- feelings

HOW TO MAINTAIN CLEAR PATIENT—PROVIDER BOUNDARIES

Define boundaries by asking:

- is this what a health provider does?

- do I sense how the patient experiences this?

- am I doing this for the patient or for me?

- are my actions supporting the health of my patient?

Strategies for maintaining boundaries:

- being patient-centered, manage feelings of personal neediness,

- monitor for transference (displacement of feelings meant for someone else that come out at the provider instead)

- monitor for countertransference (provider's feelings meant for someone else come out at the patient)

- no dual relationships

- consult with colleagues if unsure

EMPATHY BARRIERS AND HOW TO OVERCOME

Clinician barriers:

- takes too much time → make the time

- too draining → make the effort

- will lose control of interview → be confident in redirecting patient to maintain some control of the dialogue

- can't fix patient's distress → be comfortable with patients in distress

- not my job → recognize role as health care provider is to express empathy

- perceived conflict of interest → remember there is no conflict of interest in empathy if appropriate boundaries are maintained

- preference for interpreting distress in a biomedical model → remind pt they are

- welcome to share emotion

- somatization disorder → relate to pts that the experience of many emotions are a normal part of life

- desire to meet clinician's expectations

- worry about being emotionally overwhelmed → inform patient that distressing or disabling

- emotions may represent a mental health disorder that may warrant further evaluation and treatment

- lack of language for emotions → help patient identify words to express self through empathy

COMMUNICATION SKILLS: SKILLS ARE VERBAL AS WELL AS NONVERBAL

Verbal Tools:

- make acknowledgements such as mm-hmm, yeah, etc. as patient speaks

- restatement of what the patient says

- reflection of what you perceive the patient is feeling

- validation of patient's situation

- express partnership by making statements that clinician is interested in supporting the patient

- respect appropriate use of self-disclosure: when clinician expresses similarities, etc. with the intention of making the patient feel empathized with, but done in a way to not retract attention away from the patient

- making use of meaningful silences **Nonverbal Tools:**

- eye contact in moderate amounts, no staring

- facial expression: appearing interested, mirroring concept

- head nods in moderation, no bobble-heading

- maintain a 3-4 foot distance during history taking

- posture: open stance, relaxed, leaning towards patient

COMMUNICATION SKILLS ARE USED TO ASSURE DIRECT, HONEST, THERAPEUTIC COMMUNICATION WITH PATIENTS, TO EXPRESS EMPATHY, AND TO COUNSEL AND EDUCATE

How effective are you at communicating?

- intention: what response do you intend to create?

- action: what skill do you need to yield the intended response from the patient?

- response: did the patient respond as intended?

- reflection: how was the experience and what would you do to modify it?

COUNSELING SKILLS

- First: need to build a foundation with empathy and a therapeutic relationship with patient • Make use of communication tools

- Coding considerations:

- if > 50% of face to face time with patient is spent in counseling, time may be used as basis for selection of level of service (Simple Nursing)

Appendix II.A.

Tony

The following insights and conversations are all part of dialogues that occurred between my grandson, Dominick, and me within the past 4 years. These interactions have led to a strong bond between us. He has expressed his gratitude for the interest I have taken in his welfare.

Recently, Dominick, asked me what my return to New York has meant to me. I said that reuniting with my family has renewed my energy.

Dominick is passionate about baseball and football. We have had the opportunity to share thoughts about his love of the games and his future plans. Taking him to practices and games has given me the chance to witness his growth and to draw parallels in our lives.

One time, Dominick participated in an exhibition game among peers at a major league ballpark. Imagine my feelings as he came in from the bullpen and dominated the opposition. Anyone who has witnessed the good performance of a loved one can identify with my experience. I asked Dominick, "What have you learned from your participation in sports?"

Dominick:
1. When I am successful, I gain confidence.
2. I don't like failure.
3. Practice helps me improve.
4. Grandpa taught me how to use failure as a motivator.
5. I'm learning to plan ahead.
6. I like training at a gym.
7. I'd rather lead than follow.
8. Grandpa told me about his own experiences in leadership and what it took.
9. Playing sports can be risky. I accept it.

10. Success requires teamwork. I enjoy supporting my teammates.
11. I appreciate a coach who believes in me.
12. Uptight coaches create stress among the players.
13. Grandpa taught me how to talk to coaches when I disagree with them.
14. Mutual respect helps the team.
15. I benefit from good examples. I learned to say "Yes", when I mean yes, and to say "No", if I mean no.
16. I'm learning what's right for me.
17. Good coaches will place you where you can perform best.
18. Grandpa has explained why it's important to trust in yourself.
19. I like to compete.
20. I have learned how proper mechanics work together.
21. When I had difficulty in math, Grandpa suggested that I look at the problems as games to be played. Learn the theorems as if they were sports. Focus on the connections to come to the conclusion. I understood and I applied this to games like Scrabble as well math and sports.
22. Grandpa told me about his experiences when he discovered a hidden ability. He was willing to search for alternatives. I am now considering law enforcement as a possible career.
23. I don't like injustice.
24. I like donating food to the poor.

Tony

I smiled proudly when Dominick said, "I've enjoyed doing this. I hope it helps someone."

These are examples of cognitive restructuring, which are used in everyday interactions.

I used what I learned in therapy to teach Dominick many invaluable lessons.

Appendix II.B.

Anthony Jr., the second oldest of six children, chose a technical program in high school, and then pursued a career as an airline technician. He became FAA certified as an airline technician with training in airframe and powerplant discipline. These licenses allowed him to work under Federal Aviation regulations.

Years later, because of the enormous pressure of his job, he asked his father for suggestions to deal with the stress that was affecting his relationships with his wife and daughter. His colleagues called this intense anxiety a "Vesuvio Response", explosiveness in reaction to stress.

Tony suggested that he, Anthony, Jr., seek help from a cognitive behavioral therapist. Anthony agreed. Cognitive behavioral therapy and anti-anxiety medication helped Anthony Jr. learn to re-shape his debilitating, anxious thoughts.

Through therapy, Anthony Jr., discovered the triggers, which resulted in negative thinking and its ramifications. He learned to identify those triggers; he needed to learn to use the insights he gained.

The interpretations helped him deal with his stressful career. He has been promoted from technician to line technician, to supervisor, and now maintenance coordinator. Anthony Jr's insights are the result of listening to his father and working with a cognitive behavioral therapist. He became aware of the triggers that contributed to his intense anger when he was disillusioned. He had to change the way he interpreted events.

Table 4: <u>This table illustrates Anthony Jr's response process.</u> The triggers causing the anxiety, his interpretations of them, their effect on his behavior, and <u>the cognitive skill to modify his reactions can be seen in the following</u> <u>table.</u>

Triggers by duty managers	Interpretation of the event	Both effects on his behavior	Cognitive skills
staffing minimums ignored	erosion and helplessness	developing "Why should I" mentality; reluctance to adhere to dictates	doing the job correctly anyway
ignoring less motivated workers	others having to do their wok	annoyance, victimization, anger	doing what is reasonably expected
suggestions to improve operational efficiency ignored	dismissing Anthony's proposals for a more efficient way to manage	anger, resentment, disillusionment, disappointment among line workers	continuing to be proactive and persistent; possibility in the future to be heard

Anthony Jr. questioned whether he had a deep sense of responsibility similar to that of his father. He realized that, by embracing his work, he could maintain his integrity and communicate more effectively with other employees. He became proactive instead of reactive. By remaining in the present, he was able to focus on what was actually happening. Additionally, Anthony Jr. learned the importance of seeing the humorous aspects of situations and was able to use his humor to diffuse his unbridled anger. Anthony Jr. learned to access and appreciate his resourcefulness and the positive aspects of his personality.

APPENDIX II.C.
THE BENEFITS OF TONY'S RISK-TAKING
RESOLUTION THROUGH SELF-DESENSITIZATION AND UNDERSTANDING

ANECDOTE 1

Tony had an intense fear of drowning in deep water. I pointed out that most people can learn to float to gain control of their fear. He decided it was time to overcome his panic. To this end, he began to force himself to venture into the deep end of a pool. He instinctively started at the shallow end. He began dunking his head in the water to overcome his anxiety and attempted to float. He achieved his goal by taking these incremental steps. The length of time needed to desensitize himself was two weeks. He progressed by spending 2 days on each step until he mastered the behavior. Though never becoming a swimmer, Tony did become more comfortable in water. His success enabled him to help family members who were struggling in the same way.

ANECDOTE 2

Years before he started therapy with me, Tony decided to quit smoking, one of the most difficult addictive habit disturbances to give up. Prior attempts had failed. This time he had a three-week head start because of severe bronchitis. He tried to capitalize on this, but slowly his resolution weakened. We have all made New Year's resolutions to change behaviors, but we are frequently unable to follow through. By using what he knew worked with his students, he developed a protocol that allowed him to reach his goal.

Certain occasions prompted him to reach for a cigarette. While having a cup of coffee, his hand unconsciously went to his shirt pocket. The automatic nature of these behaviors, nestled in the midbrain, induces the associations made between an event and the habit, in this case smoking a cigarette. These associations encourage us to indulge the behavior. Tony reasoned that he could develop a vigilance to stop himself. The list of associations grew as he thought about his life. Tony developed his own mantra "not this time". Each time he had this thought it provided self-reinforcement. The reward strengthened his resolve to quit.

Sometimes simple solutions make difficult choices more manageable. Taking one successful day at a time prevents the problematic thinking about the future and what we have to face over a long period.

I know smokers who become so frantic when running out of cigarettes. They search everywhere for used cigarette butts in ashtrays to satisfy their yearning. An example of this is Tony's grandfather who smoked tightly packed Italian cigars. He kept the stubs in a pipe to prevent any waste.

Tony felt that he was developing the strength to avoid consuming a dangerous drug, nicotine, which was consuming him. Though Tony continued to feel some desire to smoke, even after nine months, the urges were diminishing and his resolve was strengthening. Tony was able to access his inner strength. His emotional reactions became self-awareness and a proactive resolution.

A significant turning point came after a visit to a relative who had a cancerous lung removed but still died. This visit triggered an obsessive rumination over his addiction and the harmful effects of smoking. This anecdote is one example of the usefulness of obsessive rumination. This time it helped him conquer a habit.

If we are able to use obsessions successfully, we have great difficulty believing that obsessive thoughts can be detrimental. Forty-eight years have gone by, and despite rare moments of craving a cigarette, Tony has never given in. This is one clear example of our inherent strength that we tend overlook and ignore.

Tony related this anecdote in our initial consultation. It provided me with insight into his personality and prompted me to reinforce his basic survival instinct. As I interpreted this behavior for him, Tony recognized the connection to other challenges that he had overcome in his life. He learned that he was stronger than he believed. This realization resulted in a significant change to his thinking and his behaviors.

ANECDOTE 3

Tony

I told Dr. Guido that I obsess about future events because I have difficulty with unpredictable outcomes. He pointed out that this is an embedded, learned experience involving pain.

Dr. Guido then asked me to identify experiences over which I feel I have no control. He commented on a pattern in my thought processes that dictates the order of interconnected events. When asked for an example from my past, I immediately remembered my experience speaking to a group of administrators after teaching an experimental algebra course. (V: chapter 12) As a result of my well-received presentation and encouragement from my audience, I was able to capitalize on this and become a motivational speaker several years later. This is an example of my long-held belief that there have been several events in my life that were apparently significantly related, but for which I could not determine any causal connection. As I discussed this further in therapy, I realized that there is usually a linear relationship and that I am fortunate to have the inner resources that help me make frequent connections between opportunities and success.

I taught Tony that it is up to each of us to make certain connections based in our own past. This, in turn, helps us reach resolution through cognitive restructuring.

Tony

I am more aware that incidents in life can empower me to move forward. When I survived my thoracic surgery, and the sedation necessary to calm my frenetic behavior in recovery, I understood that I might have died. I finally realized the importance of overcoming my fears and taking risks to enhance my life. I used my new-found insights to overcome my fear of public speaking and to provide religious instruction to interested adults. I also organized a weekend spiritual retreats.

abnormal -deviating from what is normal or usual, typically in a way that is undesirable or worrying

acting-out -expressing our emotional issues in defiance of what is considered appropriate behavior by various authority figures.

acute stress disorder -a temporary pattern of arousal caused by a stressor with a clear onset and offset.

adjunct -connected or added to something, typically in an auxiliary way

adrenal glands -endocrine glands that produce a wide variety of hormones

AIDS (autoimmune deficiency syndrome) -a disease in which there is a severe loss of the body's cellular immunity, a sexually transmitted disease, greatly lowering the resistance to infection and malignancy

amygdala -a roughly almond-shaped mass of gray matter inside each cerebral hemisphere, involved with the experiencing of emotions

angiotensin-converting-enzyme (ACE) inhibitors -help relax blood vessels.

antipsychotic medications -medicines that diminish psychotic symptoms usually by their effect on the dopamine pathways in the brain

anxiety disorder -mental problems characterized mainly by anxiety. Anxiety disorders include panic disorder, specific phobias. and obsessive-compulsive disorder

aphasic -a condition that robs you of the ability to communicate

archetypes -a collectively-inherited unconscious idea, pattern of thought, image, etc., that is universally present in individual psyches

autoimmune disease -diseases in which the body attacks and damages its own tissues

autonomic nervous system -the part of the nervous system responsible for control of the bodily functions not consciously directed, such as breathing, the heartbeat, and digestive processes

benign -(of a disease) not harmful in effect: in particular, (of a tumor) not malignant

beta blockers -class of drugs that are particularly used for the management of cardiac arrhythmias

bipolar disorder I -a severe mental abnormality involving swings of mood from mania to depression

bipolar disorder II -a mental abnormality involving less intense swings of mood from hypomania to depression

boundaries -a line that marks the limits of an area; a dividing line

breakdown -formerly used to describe a mental condition often requiring hospitalization

burnout -a metaphor for the exhaustive stage of stress

cardiologist -a physician who specializes in diseases of the heart

catalyst -a substance that increases the rate of a chemical reaction without itself undergoing any permanent chemical change

clinical psychologists -psychological practitioners who specialize In the treatment of mental disorders

cognitive functioning -any mental process that involves symbolic operations: perception, memory, creation of imagery, and thinking

cognitive restructuring -psychotherapeutic process of learning to identify and dispute irrational or maladaptive thoughts such as allor-nothing thinking, magical thinking, filtering, overgeneralization, magnification, and emotional reasoning. It may employs Socratic questioning, thought recording, and guided imagery and is used successfully in cognitive behavioral therapy

cognitive behavioral therapy -a type of psychotherapy in which negative patterns of thought about the self and the world are challenged in order to alter unwanted behavior patterns or treat mood disorders such as depression

conscious -aware of and responding to one's surroundings

constructive anger -anger that can be healing

critical stress intervention -adaptive, short-term psychological helping-process that focuses solely on an immediate and identifiable problem

delusions -an idiosyncratic belief or impression that is firmly maintained despite being contradicted by what is generally accepted as reality or rational argument, typically a symptom of mental disorder

denial -the action of declaring something to be untrue

dependency -a dependent or subordinate person, controlled by another

depression -feelings of severe despondency and dejection

diplomate -a person who holds a diploma, especially a doctor certified as a specialist by a board of examiners

dopamine -a compound present in the body as a neurotransmitter and a precursor of other substances including epinephrine

dysfunctional -not operating normally or properly

electroconvulsive therapy -relating to the treatment of mental illness by the application of electric shocks to the brain

empower -give someone permission to do something

enabling -give someone the authority or means to do something

endocrine glands -the body's chemical messenger system, including the pituitary, adrenals, gonads, thyroid, parathyroid, pancreas, ovaries, testes

epinephrine -another term for adrenaline

Eurocentric -focusing on European culture or history to the exclusion of a wider view of the world; implicitly regarding European culture as preeminent

exhaustive stage of stress -final stage, in which adaptive mechanisms collapse. End of this state is compete depletion of resources.

fibromyalgia -a chronic disorder characterized by widespread musculo-skeletal pain, fatigue, and tenderness in localized area

flashback -a scene from life set in a time earlier than the main story

habituated -make or become accustomed or used to something

hallucinations -an experience involving the apparent perception of something not present

hedonistic -engaged in the pursuit of pleasure; sensually self-indulgent

helicopter parent -a parent who takes an overprotective or excessive interest in the life of their child or children

hematologist -a physician concerned with the study, diagnosis, treatment, and prevention of blood diseases

hormone -a regulatory substance produced by a gland and transported in tissue fluids such as blood to stimulate specific cells or tissues into action

hypervigilance -an enhanced state of sensory sensitivity accompanied by an exaggerated intensity of behaviors whose purpose is to detect threats

hypomania –a mental state marked by elation, hyperactivity, and grandiosity

imprint -a young child comes to recognize another person as a parent or other object of habitual trust

in utero -in a woman's uterus; before birth

individuate -distinguish from others of the same kind

inertia -a tendency to do nothing or to remain unchanged

infantilize -treat someone as a child or in a way that denies their maturity in age or experience

insight -the capacity to gain an accurate and deep intuitive understanding of a person or thing

instant gratification -the satisfaction gained by more impulsive behaviors: I-wnt-what-I-want-when-I-want-it

intellectualization -a defense mechanism using reasoning to block confrontation with an unconscious conflict and its associated emotional stress; thinking is used to avoid feeling.

internalize -make attitudes or behavior part of one's nature by learning or unconscious assimilation

interpretations -the action of explaining the meaning of something

intervention -the action or process of intervening, such as family members attempting to motivate the substance abuser to enter a program designed overcome the addiction.

limbic system -a complex system of nerves and networks in the brain, involving several areas near the edge of the cortex concerned with instinct and mood. It controls the basic emotions (fear, pleasure, anger) and drives (hunger, sex, dominance, care of offspring)

lithium -a simple compound that is highly effective in dampening the extreme mood swings of bipolar disorder

lupus -any of various diseases or conditions marked by inflammation of the skin, especially lupus vulgaris or lupus erythematosus

manic-depressive illness -archaic nomenclature for bipolar disorder

mantra -a word or sound repeated to aid concentration in meditation

meningioma -a tumor that arises from the meninges — the membranes that surround your brain

midbrain -a small central part of the brainstem, developing from the middle of the primitive or embryonic brain

mood disorder -Abnormal disturbances in emotion or mood, including bipolar disorder and unipolar disorder. Mood disorders are also called *affective disorders*

multifaceted -having many parts

musculoskeletal -relating to or denoting the musculature and skeleton together

narcissism -grandiose sense of self-importance and a need For constant attention or admiration

neurologist -physician trained to diagnose and treat disorders of the nervous system.

neurotransmitter -a chemical substance that is released at the end of a nerve fiber by the arrival of a nerve impulse and, by diffusing across the synapse or junction, causes the transfer of the impulse to another nerve fiber, a muscle fiber, or some other structure

non-judgmental -avoiding moral judgments

norepinephrine -a hormone that is released by the adrenal medulla and by the sympathetic nerves and functions as a neurotransmitter

nuclear family -a couple and their dependent children, regarded as a basic social unit

obsessive -of the nature of an obsession

obsessive-compulsive disorder -a condition characterized by patterns of persistent, unwanted thoughts and behaviors

object constancy -the capacity to understand that an absent person or object exists and will return

organic roots (of psychological disorders) -looking for clues to these disorders in the tissues of the brain

overdetermined -determine, account for, or cause (something) in more than one way or with more conditions than are necessary

panic attack -a sudden feeling of acute and disabling anxiety

panic disorder -a disturbance marked by anxiety attacks that have no connection with events in the person's present experience

paranoid schizophrenia -a form of schizophrenia in which a combination of delusions and hallucinations is the prominent feature

parietal-temporal lobe -the part of the brain that integrates sensory information among various modalities

physiological -referring to the body

physiology of stress -physical manifestations of psychological stress

physiology -the branch of biology that deals with the normal functions of living organisms and their parts

positive self-esteem -gives us the strength and flexibility to take charge of our lives and grow from our mistakes without the fear of rejection

post-traumatic stress syndrome (PTSD) -may develop after exposure to one or more traumatic events, i.e., major stress, sexual assault, terrorism

proactive -creating or controlling a situation by causing something to happen rather than responding to it after it has happened

Prozac -SSRI antidepressant; affects brain chemicals that may cause depression, panic, anxiety, or obsessive-compulsive symptoms

psychiatrist -a medical practitioner specializing in the diagnosis and treatment of mental illness, often prescribing psychopharmacological drugs and/or ECT

psychoanalysis -system of psychological theory and therapy that aims to treat mental disorders by investigating the interaction of conscious and unconscious elements in the mind and bringing repressed fears and conflicts into the conscious mind by techniques such as dream interpretation and free association

psychoanalytic -the use of Freudian and non-Freudian techniques

psychodynamic -a viewpoint that emphasizes the understanding of mental disorders in terms of unconscious needs, desires, memories, and conflicts

psychological -of, affecting, or arising in the mind; related to the mental and emotional state of a person

psychologist -an expert or specialist in psychology

psychosocial development -any of the eight major developmental challenges across the lifespan, which require an individual to rethink his or her orientation to self and others (Erikson)

psychotherapy -the treatment of mental disorder by psychological rather than medical means

psychotic episodes -periods of time in which a person experiences profound disturbances in perception or affect

psychotic -of, denoting, or suffering from a psychosis

psychotropic medication -relating to or denoting drugs that affect a person's mental state

quid pro quo -a favor or advantage granted or expected in return for something

reality-oriented psychotherapy -focuses on the here-and-now actions of the client and the ability to create and choose a better future

remission -the cancellation of a symptom

repetition-compulsion -psychological phenomenon in which a person repeats or reenacts a traumatic event or its circumstances over and over again, including putting oneself in situations where the event is likely to happen again

resistance -the refusal to accept or comply with something; the attempt to prevent something by action or argument

rheumatoid arthritis -a chronic progressive disease causing inflammation in the joints and resulting in painful deformity and immobility, especially in the fingers, wrists, feet, and ankles.

role model -a person looked to by others as an example to be imitated

schizophrenia -a long-term mental disorder of a type involving a breakdown in the relation between thought, emotion, and behavior, leading to faulty perception, inappropriate actions and feelings, withdrawal from reality and personal relationships into fantasy and delusion, and a sense of mental fragmentation

seasonal affective disorder (SAD) -a form of depression and/or elation reactive to deprivation of and/or increases in sunlight that cause alterations to brain chemistry

secondary gain -exaggerating symptoms for personal gain

self-actualization -the highest plateau that one can reach in Maslow's Hierarchy of Needs

self-defeating -of an action unable, because of its inherent qualities, to achieve the end it is designed to bring about

self-discovery -the process of acquiring insight into one's own character

self-gratification -the indulgence or satisfaction of one's own desires

separation anxiety -anxiety provoked in a children and adults reacting to threat of separation from a significant other

separation -the action or state of moving or being moved apart

serotonin -a compound present in blood platelets and serum that constricts the blood vessels and acts as a neurotransmitter

selective serotonin reuptake inhibitors (SSRI) -a class of compounds typically used as antidepressants in the treatment of major depressive disorder and anxiety disorders

socio-cultural changes -a path to self-understanding of cultural and social evolution over time.

STD -a sexually transmitted disease.

subconscious -the subconscious part of the mind (not in technical use in psychoanalysis, where unconscious is preferred)

symbiotic relationship -a relationship between two people or groups that work with and depend on each other

sympathetic nervous system -stimulates the body's fight-or-flight response

temperament -a person's nature, especially as it permanently affects her/his behavior

temporal arteritis -inflammation and damage to the blood vessels that supply blood to the head

therapist -a person skilled in a particular kind of therapy. Synonyms: psychologist, psychotherapist, analyst, counselor, psychoanalyst, psychiatrist

thyroid gland -a large ductless gland in the neck that secretes hormones regulating growth and development through the rate of metabolism.

unconscious -the part of the mind that is inaccessible to the conscious mind but that affects behavior and emotions..

Venn diagram -a diagram representing logical sets pictorially as circles, common elements of the sets being represented by the areas of overlap

Stephen M. Guido, PhD, is a clinical psychologist who received his doctorate from St. John's University. Dr. Guido has been in practice for more than forty-five years. He is located in Commack, New York, and he invites you to visit his website: www.drstephenmguido.com

Dr. Guido is a cognitive behavioral therapist. He works with patients ranging from young children through senior citizens. Specializing in trauma and stress management, he is an expert in the treatment of ADD, OCD, phobias, panic disorder, mood disorder, personality disorder, and family and/or couples issues. He has taught university courses, participated in local television interviews, and served as vice president and clinical director of a corporate consulting firm. Written to take the mystery and stigma out of psychotherapy, *Between the Lines* is his first book.

Anthony Terracciano received an MA in education from SUNY Stony Brook. Mr. Terracciano is a retired public school math teacher who has shared his therapeutic journey in collaboration with Dr. Guido to help others address their psychological issues. He would like readers to understand that they can attain peace of mind through therapy.

www.ingramcontent.com/pod-product-compliance
Lightning Source LLC
Chambersburg PA
CBHW071039290526
45795CB00004B/1221